STAAR

Success Strategies
Grade 8 Social Studies

DEAR FUTURE EXAM SUCCESS STORY

First of all, **THANK YOU** for purchasing Mometrix study materials!

Second, congratulations! You are one of the few determined test-takers who are committed to doing whatever it takes to excel on your exam. **You have come to the right place.** We developed these study materials with one goal in mind: to deliver you the information you need in a format that's concise and easy to use.

In addition to optimizing your guide for the content of the test, we've outlined our recommended steps for breaking down the preparation process into small, attainable goals so you can make sure you stay on track.

We've also analyzed the entire test-taking process, identifying the most common pitfalls and showing how you can overcome them and be ready for any curveball the test throws you.

Standardized testing is one of the biggest obstacles on your road to success, which only increases the importance of doing well in the high-pressure, high-stakes environment of test day. Your results on this test could have a significant impact on your future, and this guide provides the information and practical advice to help you achieve your full potential on test day.

Your success is our success

We would love to hear from you! If you would like to share the story of your exam success or if you have any questions or comments in regard to our products, please contact us at **800-673-8175** or **support@mometrix.com**.

Thanks again for your business and we wish you continued success!

Sincerely,
The Mometrix Test Preparation Team

Need more help? Check out our flashcards at: http://MometrixFlashcards.com/STAAR

TABLE OF CONTENTS

Introduction

Thank you for purchasing this resource! You have made the choice to prepare yourself for a test that could have a huge impact on your future, and this guide is designed to help you be fully ready for test day. Obviously, it's important to have a solid understanding of the test material, but you also need to be prepared for the unique environment and stressors of the test, so that you can perform to the best of your abilities.

For this purpose, the first section that appears in this guide is the **Success Strategies**. We've devoted countless hours to meticulously researching what works and what doesn't, and we've boiled down our findings to the five most impactful steps you can take to improve your performance on the test. We start at the beginning with study planning and move through the preparation process, all the way to the testing strategies that will help you get the most out of what you know when you're finally sitting in front of the test.

We recommend that you start preparing for your test as far in advance as possible. However, if you've bought this guide as a last-minute study resource and only have a few days before your test, we recommend that you skip over the first two Success Strategies since they address a long-term study plan.

If you struggle with **test anxiety**, we strongly encourage you to check out our recommendations for how you can overcome it. Test anxiety is a formidable foe, but it can be beaten, and we want to make sure you have the tools you need to defeat it.

Strategy #1 – Plan Big, Study Small

There's a lot riding on your performance. If you want to ace this test, you're going to need to keep your skills sharp and the material fresh in your mind. You need a plan that lets you review everything you need to know while still fitting in your schedule. We'll break this strategy down into three categories.

Information Organization

Start with the information you already have: the official test outline. From this, you can make a complete list of all the concepts you need to cover before the test. Organize these concepts into groups that can be studied together, and create a list of any related vocabulary you need to learn so you can brush up on any difficult terms. You'll want to keep this vocabulary list handy once you actually start studying since you may need to add to it along the way.

Time Management

Once you have your set of study concepts, decide how to spread them out over the time you have left before the test. Break your study plan into small, clear goals so you have a manageable task for each day and know exactly what you're doing. Then just focus on one small step at a time. When you manage your time this way, you don't need to spend hours at a time studying. Studying a small block of content for a short period each day helps you retain information better and avoid stressing over how much you have left to do. You can relax knowing that you have a plan to cover everything in time. In order for this strategy to be effective though, you have to start studying early and stick to your schedule. Avoid the exhaustion and futility that comes from last-minute cramming!

Study Environment

The environment you study in has a big impact on your learning. Studying in a coffee shop, while probably more enjoyable, is not likely to be as fruitful as studying in a quiet room. It's important to keep distractions to a minimum. You're only planning to study for a short block of time, so make the most of it. Don't pause to check your phone or get up to find a snack. It's also important to **avoid multitasking**. Research has consistently shown that multitasking will make your studying dramatically less effective. Your study area should also be comfortable and well-lit so you don't have the distraction of straining your eyes or sitting on an uncomfortable chair.

 The time of day you study is also important. You want to be rested and alert. Don't wait until just before bedtime. Study when you'll be most likely to comprehend and remember. Even better, if you know what time of day your test will be, set that time aside for study. That way your brain will be used to working on that subject at that specific time and you'll have a better chance of recalling information.

Finally, it can be helpful to team up with others who are studying for the same test. Your actual studying should be done in as isolated an environment as possible, but the work of organizing the information and setting up the study plan can be divided up. In between study sessions, you can discuss with your teammates the concepts that you're all studying and quiz each other on the details. Just be sure that your teammates are as serious about the test as you are. If you find that your study time is being replaced with social time, you might need to find a new team.

Strategy #2 – Make Your Studying Count

You're devoting a lot of time and effort to preparing for this test, so you want to be absolutely certain it will pay off. This means doing more than just reading the content and hoping you can remember it on test day. It's important to make every minute of study count. There are two main areas you can focus on to make your studying count.

Retention

It doesn't matter how much time you study if you can't remember the material. You need to make sure you are retaining the concepts. To check your retention of the information you're learning, try recalling it at later times with minimal prompting. Try carrying around flashcards and glance at one or two from time to time or ask a friend who's also studying for the test to quiz you.

To enhance your retention, look for ways to put the information into practice so that you can apply it rather than simply recalling it. If you're using the information in practical ways, it will be much easier to remember. Similarly, it helps to solidify a concept in your mind if you're not only reading it to yourself but also explaining it to someone else. Ask a friend to let you teach them about a concept you're a little shaky on (or speak aloud to an imaginary audience if necessary). As you try to summarize, define, give examples, and answer your friend's questions, you'll understand the concepts better and they will stay with you longer. Finally, step back for a big picture view and ask yourself how each piece of information fits with the whole subject. When you link the different concepts together and see them working together as a whole, it's easier to remember the individual components.

Finally, practice showing your work on any multi-step problems, even if you're just studying. Writing out each step you take to solve a problem will help solidify the process in your mind, and you'll be more likely to remember it during the test.

Modality

Modality simply refers to the means or method by which you study. Choosing a study modality that fits your own individual learning style is crucial. No two people learn best in exactly the same way, so it's important to know your strengths and use them to your advantage.

For example, if you learn best by visualization, focus on visualizing a concept in your mind and draw an image or a diagram. Try color-coding your notes, illustrating them, or creating symbols that will trigger your mind to recall a learned concept. If you learn best by hearing or discussing information, find a study partner who learns the same way or read aloud to yourself. Think about how to put the information in your own words. Imagine that you are giving a lecture on the topic and record yourself so you can listen to it later.

For any learning style, flashcards can be helpful. Organize the information so you can take advantage of spare moments to review. Underline key words or phrases. Use different colors for different categories. Mnemonic devices (such as creating a short list in which every item starts with the same letter) can also help with retention. Find what works best for you and use it to store the information in your mind most effectively and easily.

3

Strategy #3 – Practice the Right Way

Your success on test day depends not only on how many hours you put into preparing, but also on whether you prepared the right way. It's good to check along the way to see if your studying is paying off. One of the most effective ways to do this is by taking practice tests to evaluate your progress. Practice tests are useful because they show exactly where you need to improve. Every time you take a practice test, pay special attention to these three groups of questions:

- The questions you got wrong
- The questions you had to guess on, even if you guessed right
- The questions you found difficult or slow to work through

This will show you exactly what your weak areas are, and where you need to devote more study time. Ask yourself why each of these questions gave you trouble. Was it because you didn't understand the material? Was it because you didn't remember the vocabulary? Do you need more repetitions on this type of question to build speed and confidence? Dig into those questions and figure out how you can strengthen your weak areas as you go back to review the material.

 Additionally, many practice tests have a section explaining the answer choices. It can be tempting to read the explanation and think that you now have a good understanding of the concept. However, an explanation likely only covers part of the question's broader context. Even if the explanation makes perfect sense, **go back and investigate** every concept related to the question until you're positive you have a thorough understanding.

As you go along, keep in mind that the practice test is just that: practice. Memorizing these questions and answers will not be very helpful on the actual test because it is unlikely to have any of the same exact questions. If you only know the right answers to the sample questions, you won't be prepared for the real thing. **Study the concepts** until you understand them fully, and then you'll be able to answer any question that shows up on the test.

It's important to wait on the practice tests until you're ready. If you take a test on your first day of study, you may be overwhelmed by the amount of material covered and how much you need to learn. Work up to it gradually.

On test day, you'll need to be prepared for answering questions, managing your time, and using the test-taking strategies you've learned. It's a lot to balance, like a mental marathon that will have a big impact on your future. Like training for a marathon, you'll need to start slowly and work your way up. When test day arrives, you'll be ready.

Start with the strategies you've read in the first two Success Strategies—plan your course and study in the way that works best for you. If you have time, consider using multiple study resources to get different approaches to the same concepts. It can be helpful to see difficult concepts from more than one angle. Then find a good source for practice tests. Many times, the test website will suggest potential study resources or provide sample tests.

Practice Test Strategy

If you're able to find at least three practice tests, we recommend this strategy:

UNTIMED AND OPEN-BOOK PRACTICE

Take the first test with no time constraints and with your notes and study guide handy. Take your time and focus on applying the strategies you've learned.

TIMED AND OPEN-BOOK PRACTICE

Take the second practice test open-book as well, but set a timer and practice pacing yourself to finish in time.

TIMED AND CLOSED-BOOK PRACTICE

Take any other practice tests as if it were test day. Set a timer and put away your study materials. Sit at a table or desk in a quiet room, imagine yourself at the testing center, and answer questions as quickly and accurately as possible.

Keep repeating timed and closed-book tests on a regular basis until you run out of practice tests or it's time for the actual test. Your mind will be ready for the schedule and stress of test day, and you'll be able to focus on recalling the material you've learned.

Strategy #4 – Pace Yourself

Once you're fully prepared for the material on the test, your biggest challenge on test day will be managing your time. Just knowing that the clock is ticking can make you panic even if you have plenty of time left. Work on pacing yourself so you can build confidence against the time constraints of the exam. Pacing is a difficult skill to master, especially in a high-pressure environment, so **practice is vital**.

Set time expectations for your pace based on how much time is available. For example, if a section has 60 questions and the time limit is 30 minutes, you know you have to average 30 seconds or less per question in order to answer them all. Although 30 seconds is the hard limit, set 25 seconds per question as your goal, so you reserve extra time to spend on harder questions. When you budget extra time for the harder questions, you no longer have any reason to stress when those questions take longer to answer.

Don't let this time expectation distract you from working through the test at a calm, steady pace, but keep it in mind so you don't spend too much time on any one question. Recognize that taking extra time on one question you don't understand may keep you from answering two that you do understand later in the test. If your time limit for a question is up and you're still not sure of the answer, mark it and move on, and come back to it later if the time and the test format allow. If the testing format doesn't allow you to return to earlier questions, just make an educated guess; then put it out of your mind and move on.

On the easier questions, be careful not to rush. It may seem wise to hurry through them so you have more time for the challenging ones, but it's not worth missing one if you know the concept and just didn't take the time to read the question fully. Work efficiently but make sure you understand the question and have looked at all of the answer choices, since more than one may seem right at first.

Even if you're paying attention to the time, you may find yourself a little behind at some point. You should speed up to get back on track, but do so wisely. Don't panic; just take a few seconds less on each question until you're caught up. Don't guess without thinking, but do look through the answer choices and eliminate any you know are wrong. If you can get down to two choices, it is often worthwhile to guess from those. Once you've chosen an answer, move on and don't dwell on any that you skipped or had to hurry through. If a question was taking too long, chances are it was one of the harder ones, so you weren't as likely to get it right anyway.

On the other hand, if you find yourself getting ahead of schedule, it may be beneficial to slow down a little. The more quickly you work, the more likely you are to make a careless mistake that will affect your score. You've budgeted time for each question, so don't be afraid to spend that time. Practice an efficient but careful pace to get the most out of the time you have.

Test-Taking Strategies

This section contains a list of test-taking strategies that you may find helpful as you work through the test. By taking what you know and applying logical thought, you can maximize your chances of answering any question correctly!

It is very important to realize that every question is different and every person is different: no single strategy will work on every question, and no single strategy will work for every person. That's why we've included all of them here, so you can try them out and determine which ones work best for different types of questions and which ones work best for you.

Question Strategies

⊘ READ CAREFULLY

Read the question and the answer choices carefully. Don't miss the question because you misread the terms. You have plenty of time to read each question thoroughly and make sure you understand what is being asked. Yet a happy medium must be attained, so don't waste too much time. You must read carefully and efficiently.

⊘ CONTEXTUAL CLUES

Look for contextual clues. If the question includes a word you are not familiar with, look at the immediate context for some indication of what the word might mean. Contextual clues can often give you all the information you need to decipher the meaning of an unfamiliar word. Even if you can't determine the meaning, you may be able to narrow down the possibilities enough to make a solid guess at the answer to the question.

⊘ PREFIXES

If you're having trouble with a word in the question or answer choices, try dissecting it. Take advantage of every clue that the word might include. Prefixes can be a huge help. Usually, they allow you to determine a basic meaning. *Pre-* means before, *post-* means after, *pro-* is positive, *de-* is negative. From prefixes, you can get an idea of the general meaning of the word and try to put it into context.

⊘ HEDGE WORDS

Watch out for critical hedge words, such as *likely, may, can, sometimes, often, almost, mostly, usually, generally, rarely,* and *sometimes.* Question writers insert these hedge phrases to cover every possibility. Often an answer choice will be wrong simply because it leaves no room for exception. Be on guard for answer choices that have definitive words such as *exactly* and *always.*

⊘ SWITCHBACK WORDS

Stay alert for *switchbacks.* These are the words and phrases frequently used to alert you to shifts in thought. The most common switchback words are *but, although,* and *however.* Others include *nevertheless, on the other hand, even though, while, in spite of, despite,* and *regardless of.* Switchback words are important to catch because they can change the direction of the question or an answer choice.

⊘ Face Value

When in doubt, use common sense. Accept the situation in the problem at face value. Don't read too much into it. These problems will not require you to make wild assumptions. If you have to go beyond creativity and warp time or space in order to have an answer choice fit the question, then you should move on and consider the other answer choices. These are normal problems rooted in reality. The applicable relationship or explanation may not be readily apparent, but it is there for you to figure out. Use your common sense to interpret anything that isn't clear.

Answer Choice Strategies

⊘ Answer Selection

The most thorough way to pick an answer choice is to identify and eliminate wrong answers until only one is left, then confirm it is the correct answer. Sometimes an answer choice may immediately seem right, but be careful. The test writers will usually put more than one reasonable answer choice on each question, so take a second to read all of them and make sure that the other choices are not equally obvious. As long as you have time left, it is better to read every answer choice than to pick the first one that looks right without checking the others.

⊘ Answer Choice Families

An answer choice family consists of two (in rare cases, three) answer choices that are very similar in construction and cannot all be true at the same time. If you see two answer choices that are direct opposites or parallels, one of them is usually the correct answer. For instance, if one answer choice says that quantity x increases and another either says that quantity x decreases (opposite) or says that quantity y increases (parallel), then those answer choices would fall into the same family. An answer choice that doesn't match the construction of the answer choice family is more likely to be incorrect. Most questions will not have answer choice families, but when they do appear, you should be prepared to recognize them.

⊘ Eliminate Answers

Eliminate answer choices as soon as you realize they are wrong, but make sure you consider all possibilities. If you are eliminating answer choices and realize that the last one you are left with is also wrong, don't panic. Start over and consider each choice again. There may be something you missed the first time that you will realize on the second pass.

⊘ Avoid Fact Traps

Don't be distracted by an answer choice that is factually true but doesn't answer the question. You are looking for the choice that answers the question. Stay focused on what the question is asking for so you don't accidentally pick an answer that is true but incorrect. Always go back to the question and make sure the answer choice you've selected actually answers the question and is not merely a true statement.

⊘ Extreme Statements

In general, you should avoid answers that put forth extreme actions as standard practice or proclaim controversial ideas as established fact. An answer choice that states the "process should be used in certain situations, if..." is much more likely to be correct than one that states the "process should be discontinued completely." The first is a calm rational statement and doesn't even make a definitive, uncompromising stance, using a hedge word *if* to provide wiggle room, whereas the second choice is far more extreme.

8

⊘ Benchmark

As you read through the answer choices and you come across one that seems to answer the question well, mentally select that answer choice. This is not your final answer, but it's the one that will help you evaluate the other answer choices. The one that you selected is your benchmark or standard for judging each of the other answer choices. Every other answer choice must be compared to your benchmark. That choice is correct until proven otherwise by another answer choice beating it. If you find a better answer, then that one becomes your new benchmark. Once you've decided that no other choice answers the question as well as your benchmark, you have your final answer.

⊘ Predict the Answer

Before you even start looking at the answer choices, it is often best to try to predict the answer. When you come up with the answer on your own, it is easier to avoid distractions and traps because you will know exactly what to look for. The right answer choice is unlikely to be word-for-word what you came up with, but it should be a close match. Even if you are confident that you have the right answer, you should still take the time to read each option before moving on.

General Strategies

⊘ Tough Questions

If you are stumped on a problem or it appears too hard or too difficult, don't waste time. Move on! Remember though, if you can quickly check for obviously incorrect answer choices, your chances of guessing correctly are greatly improved. Before you completely give up, at least try to knock out a couple of possible answers. Eliminate what you can and then guess at the remaining answer choices before moving on.

⊘ Check Your Work

Since you will probably not know every term listed and the answer to every question, it is important that you get credit for the ones that you do know. Don't miss any questions through careless mistakes. If at all possible, try to take a second to look back over your answer selection and make sure you've selected the correct answer choice and haven't made a costly careless mistake (such as marking an answer choice that you didn't mean to mark). This quick double check should more than pay for itself in caught mistakes for the time it costs.

⊘ Pace Yourself

It's easy to be overwhelmed when you're looking at a page full of questions; your mind is confused and full of random thoughts, and the clock is ticking down faster than you would like. Calm down and maintain the pace that you have set for yourself. Especially as you get down to the last few minutes of the test, don't let the small numbers on the clock make you panic. As long as you are on track by monitoring your pace, you are guaranteed to have time for each question.

⊘ Don't Rush

It is very easy to make errors when you are in a hurry. Maintaining a fast pace in answering questions is pointless if it makes you miss questions that you would have gotten right otherwise. Test writers like to include distracting information and wrong answers that seem right. Taking a little extra time to avoid careless mistakes can make all the difference in your test score. Find a pace that allows you to be confident in the answers that you select.

9

⊘ Keep Moving

Panicking will not help you pass the test, so do your best to stay calm and keep moving. Taking deep breaths and going through the answer elimination steps you practiced can help to break through a stress barrier and keep your pace.

Final Notes

The combination of a solid foundation of content knowledge and the confidence that comes from practicing your plan for applying that knowledge is the key to maximizing your performance on test day. As your foundation of content knowledge is built up and strengthened, you'll find that the strategies included in this chapter become more and more effective in helping you quickly sift through the distractions and traps of the test to isolate the correct answer.

Now that you're preparing to move forward into the test content chapters of this book, be sure to keep your goal in mind. As you read, think about how you will be able to apply this information on the test. If you've already seen sample questions for the test and you have an idea of the question format and style, try to come up with questions of your own that you can answer based on what you're reading. This will give you valuable practice applying your knowledge in the same ways you can expect to on test day.

Good luck and good studying!

Social Studies

History

EXPLORATION AND COLONIZATION

JAMESTOWN

The first permanent English settlement, Jamestown, was established in North America in 1607. The Virginia Company of London started the colony and named it after King James I of England. Several factors contributed to the establishment of the colony. England and Spain were experiencing a period of peace. The Virginia Company provided financial support for colonization and was able to find willing settlers. Those settlers were lured by the prospects of adventure and religious freedom. In addition, they were able to continue being English subjects.

> **Review Video: When was Jamestown Founded?**
> Visit mometrix.com/academy and enter code: 881040

AGE OF EXPLORATION

The Age of Exploration is also called the **Age of Discovery**. It is generally considered to have begun in the early 15th century and continued into the 17th century. Major developments of the **Age of Exploration** included technological advances in navigation, mapmaking, and shipbuilding. These advances led to expanded European exploration of the rest of the world. Explorers set out from several European countries, including Portugal, Spain, France, and England, seeking new routes to Asia. These efforts led to the discovery of new lands, as well as colonization in India, Asia, Africa, and North America.

> **Review Video: Age of Exploration**
> Visit mometrix.com/academy and enter code: 612972

FRENCH, SPANISH, DUTCH, AND BRITISH GOALS IN COLONIZATION OF THE AMERICAS

France, Spain, the Netherlands, and England each had specific goals in the colonization of the Americas:

- Initial **French colonies** were focused on expanding the fur trade. Later, French colonization led to the growth of plantations in Louisiana, which brought numerous African slaves to the New World.
- **Spanish colonists** came to look for wealth and to convert the natives to Christianity. For some, the desire for gold led to mining in the New World, while others established large ranches.
- The **Dutch** were also involved in the fur trade and imported slaves as the need for laborers increased.
- **British colonists** arrived with various goals. Some were simply looking for additional income, while others were fleeing Britain to escape religious persecution.

> **Review Video: Colonization of the Americas**
> Visit mometrix.com/academy and enter code: 438412

ORIGINAL 13 COLONIES

REASONS FOR THE ESTABLISHMENT

The original 13 colonies were started by settlers from England. These people came to the New World for many reasons, including political ideology, economic prospects, and social change. People who disagreed with Britain's policies may have wanted to start a new society. Companies wanted to own land in the Americas as a way to increase profits. Settlers who came for economic reasons thought they could make money on goods not found in Europe, like tobacco. Many others came for social reasons, the most important of which was religious freedom.

REPRESENTATIVE GOVERNMENT

A representative government allows the people to choose who will represent them in governmental decisions. Each colony was given the opportunity to choose representatives, an action that is the mainstay of American democracy to this day. The colonists did not like the tariffs imposed upon them by King George III and did not want a system without checks and balances to occur in the colonies. A representative government allowed the colonists to keep the interests of the people in mind, rather than impose laws produced by a monarchy. Citizens could vote on candidates that would vote for them on the local, state, and federal level, since most citizens had other jobs to attend to. Representatives could be voted out of office if they did not represent the interests of the people. This allowed colonists to have a means of control over tariffs and laws that affected their own lives.

MAYFLOWER COMPACT

The Mayflower Compact of 1620 was the governing document of Plymouth Colony. The Pilgrims who came to North America aboard the *Mayflower* created the document to help organize their community. All 41 of the adult males signed the contract. The settlers knew that previous colonies had failed due to lack of government. The major idea of the compact was that the colony was to be free of English rule and that the colonists would create their own government. The Mayflower Compact was important because it was the first document to establish a community on North America that did not feel allegiance to the King of England. The central idea of self-rule paved the way for the American Revolution.

> **Review Video: What was the Purpose of the Mayflower Compact?**
> Visit mometrix.com/academy and enter code: 275859

VIRGINIA HOUSE OF BURGESSES

The Virginia House of Burgesses was the first elected legislative body in North America. The word *burgess* refers to a municipal official or a representative of a borough, as it was used in the English House of Commons. The House of Burgesses was established by the Virginia Company, the same private company that founded the Virginia Colony, under a royal charter. On July 30, 1619, the House held its first legislative assembly, but it only lasted six days due to an outbreak of malaria.

FUNDAMENTAL ORDERS OF CONNECTICUT

The Fundamental Orders of Connecticut documented the structure of the government of the Connecticut Colony. They were adopted by the Connecticut Colony council in 1639. They are considered by many historians to be the first written constitution of a Western civilization. This is why Connecticut holds the state nickname of *The Constitution State.* The Orders are a short document, but contain several of the same principles that were later used in drafting the US Constitution. The Orders state the powers of the government as well as the rights of the individual, and how those rights are ensured by the government.

REVOLUTIONARY AND CONSTITUTIONAL ERAS
MERCANTILISM AT THE TIME OF THE AGE OF EXPLORATION

As foreign trade became the most important part of every nation's economy, the economic theory of **mercantilism** became popular. According to mercantilism, a nation should never import more than it exports. Of course, it is impossible for every country to achieve this goal at the same time, so European countries were in fierce competition at all times. The solution that most nations pursued was to establish **colonies**, because these could supply resources for export by the mother country without really being considered imports. This rush to colonize had disastrous consequences for the indigenous peoples of the Americas and Africa. Europeans often looted the Native Americans for anything of value, and their need for cheap labor to cultivate the land there spawned the **African slave trade**.

CAUSES OF THE AMERICAN REVOLUTION

Colonists became increasingly frustrated with Britain's policies. After the French and Indian War, Britain badly needed money. King George III was seeking to increase revenues, and this usually meant more taxes for the colonists. In addition, the Proclamation of 1763 forbade colonists from settling west of the Appalachian Mountains. Many colonists thought this unfairly limited their economic pursuits. Tensions regarding land and taxation continued to grow at a time when John Locke's ideas on natural rights and the social contract became popular. Locke argued that people allow the government to govern them and if the government becomes tyrannical and takes away natural rights, the people have the right to rebel. All of these were factors in the colonists revolting against the British government.

COLONIAL GOVERNMENT AND BRITISH GOVERNMENT DIFFERENCES THAT LED TO "NO TAXATION WITHOUT REPRESENTATION"

As new towns and other legislative districts developed in America, the colonists began to practice **representative government**. Colonial legislative bodies were made up of elected representatives chosen by male property owners in the districts. These individuals represented the interests of the districts from which they had been elected.

By contrast, in Britain, the **Parliament** represented the entire country. Parliament was not elected to represent individual districts. Instead, they represented specific classes. Because of this drastically different approach to government, the British did not understand the colonists' statement that they had no representation in the British Parliament.

ACTS OF BRITISH PARLIAMENT THAT OCCURRED AFTER THE FRENCH AND INDIAN WARS

After the French and Indian Wars, the British Parliament passed four major acts:

1. The **Sugar Act**, 1764—this act not only required taxes to be collected on molasses brought into the colonies but gave British officials the right to search the homes of anyone suspected of violating it.
2. The **Stamp Act**, 1765—this act taxed printed materials such as newspapers and legal documents. Protests led the Stamp Act to be repealed in 1766, but the repeal also included the Declaratory Act, which stated that Parliament had the right to govern the colonies.
3. The **Quartering Act**, 1765—this act required colonists to provide accommodations and supplies for British troops. In addition, colonists were prohibited from settling west of the Appalachians until given permission by Britain.
4. The **Townshend Acts**, 1767—these acts taxed paper, paint, lead, and tea that came into the colonies. Colonists led boycotts in protest, and in Massachusetts leaders like Samuel and John Adams began to organize resistance against British rule.

FACTORS THAT LED TO THE BOSTON MASSACRE

With the passage of the **Stamp Act**, nine colonies met in New York to demand its repeal. Elsewhere, protest arose in New York City, Philadelphia, Boston, and other cities. These protests sometimes escalated into violence, often targeting ruling British officials. The passage of the **Townshend Acts** in 1767 led to additional tension in the colonies. The British sent troops to New York City and Boston. On March 5, 1770, protesters began to taunt the British troops, throwing snowballs. The soldiers responded by firing into the crowd. This clash between protesters and soldiers led to five deaths and eight injuries, and was christened the **Boston Massacre**. Shortly thereafter, Britain repealed the majority of the Townshend Acts.

TEA ACT THAT LED TO THE BOSTON TEA PARTY

The majority of the **Townshend Acts** were repealed after the Boston Massacre in 1770, but Britain kept the tax on tea. In 1773, the **Tea Act** was passed. This allowed the East India Company to sell tea for much lower prices and also allowed them to bypass American distributors, selling directly to shopkeepers instead. Colonial tea merchants saw this as a direct assault on their business. In December of 1773, the **Sons of Liberty** boarded ships in Boston Harbor and dumped 342 chests of tea into the sea in protest of the new laws. This act of protest came to be known as the **Boston Tea Party**.

COERCIVE ACTS PASSED AFTER THE BOSTON TEA PARTY

The Coercive Acts passed by Britain in 1774 were meant to punish Massachusetts for defying British authority. The following were also known as the **Intolerable Acts**:

- Shut down ports in Boston until the city paid back the value of the tea destroyed during the Boston Tea Party
- Required that local government officials in Massachusetts be appointed by the governor rather than being elected by the people
- Allowed trials of British soldiers to be transferred to Britain rather than being held in Massachusetts
- Required locals to provide lodging for British soldiers any time there was a disturbance, even if lodging required them to stay in private homes

These acts led to the assembly of the First Continental Congress in Philadelphia on September 5, 1774. Fifty-five delegates met, representing 12 of the American colonies. They sought compromise with England over England's increasingly harsh efforts to control the colonies.

ABIGAIL ADAMS

Abigail Adams, wife of John Adams, was the second First Lady of the United States and the mother of John Quincy Adams, the sixth President. Her life is one of the most well-documented of any of the early first ladies, due mainly to her extensively preserved written correspondence with her husband, who frequently sought her advice on all manner of topics related to government and politics. Adams was a prominent advocate of women's rights. She believed that women deserved more opportunities, particularly with regard to education and bettering themselves intellectually.

JOHN ADAMS

John Adams became the second president of the United States in the election of 1796; his opponent, Thomas Jefferson, became vice president because he received the second-most electoral votes. Adams was immediately confronted by the French, who were angry about the Jay Treaty and the broken Treaty of Alliance of 1788. After the French began destroying American ships, Adams sent American diplomats to meet with the French ambassador Talleyrand, who demanded tribute and

14

then snubbed the Americans. There followed an undeclared naval war between 1798 and 1800. During which, the American military grew rapidly, warships were built and the Department of the Navy was established. Finally, at the Convention of 1800, the Treaty of Alliance of 1778 was torn up and it was agreed in this new Treaty of Mortefontaine that the Americans would pay for damages done to their ships by the French, among a host of other clauses including each country giving the other Most Favored Nation trade status.

WENTWORTH CHESWELL

Wentworth Cheswell was an African-American teacher and veteran of the Revolutionary War, who served in several positions in the local government of Newmarket, New Hampshire. Despite being only one-quarter African and being listed in the census as white, Cheswell is commonly regarded as the first African-American to be elected to a public office in the state of New Hampshire. In 1768, he was elected to his first public office as a constable. This began a stretch of nearly 50 years of public service, ending with his death in 1817. Cheswell was elected to public office almost every year for the rest of his life.

SAMUEL ADAMS

Samuel Adams was one of the leaders of the American Revolution, and one of the key minds behind the political philosophies that shaped the United States government. He graduated from Harvard College but was an unsuccessful businessman before he began concentrating on a career in politics. He held various positions in colonial Massachusetts and later in the Massachusetts state government including Governor, Lieutenant Governor, and President of the Senate. As an influential political figure, he was instrumental in convincing the Continental Congress to issue the Declaration of Independence. He was also adept at swaying public opinion, using his influence to stir up anger against the British for their violations of the colonists' liberty.

MERCY OTIS WARREN

Mercy Otis Warren was a female political writer during the time of the American Revolution. She wrote on topics such as politics and war, which at the time were considered to be the domain of men. She had no formal education, but was nonetheless a great thinker and writer. At the time, there were few people who were qualified to address subjects such as these, which allowed her a niche. She did most of her political writing under the pseudonym "A Columbian Patriot," but in 1790, she published a collection of poems and plays under her real name. In 1805, she published the first history of the Revolution authored by a woman, a three-volume book titled *History of the Rise, Progress, and Termination of the American Revolution*.

JAMES ARMISTEAD

James Armistead was born as a slave but eventually gained permission to serve as a member of the Continental Army in 1781 stationed under the Marquis de Lafayette—a friend of George Washington and the commander of the French allied forces. Lafayette was gaining heavy losses from Cornwallis's troops, and he was determined to capture the infamous traitor, Benedict Arnold. At the order of Lafayette, James Armistead infiltrated the British army through Arnold's camp by posing as a runaway slave. Having spent many years in the area, he had gained a great amount of knowledge concerning the layout of the land, and the British forces were keen to use his intelligence for their purposes. Cornwallis and Arnold tasked him with spying on the colonies, which made his job of traveling back and forth between the camps even easier. James was able to discreetly supply Lafayette information about the British while feeding bad intel back to Cornwallis. Armistead's information gave Lafayette and Washington an opening to siege Cornwallis at Yorktown which led to his eventual surrender and the end of the Revolutionary War.

BENJAMIN FRANKLIN

Benjamin Franklin was one of the Founding Fathers of the United States of America. Among many other things, Franklin was in favor of colonial unity and thought the colonies should band together to create an independent nation. During the American Revolution, Franklin was a diplomat who went to Europe and worked to secure France's support for the colonists seeking independence from Britain. Without the support of France, the colonists would not have successfully gained independence. Franklin's work was instrumental in the development of the United States of America. Only a month after his return from France, Benjamin Franklin helped draft the Declaration of Independence.

CRISPUS ATTUCKS

Crispus Attucks is considered to be one of the first martyrs of the Revolutionary War. In 1770, a crowd of angry American colonists were harassing British soldiers before they were fired upon in what came to be known as the Boston Massacre. A total of five colonists were shot and killed before the violence had ended. The first to die was a sailor and rope worker named Crispus Attucks whose death became a rally cry for American independence. Even though Attucks was an escaped slave, his death still became a symbol of heroism and patriotism employed by the colonists and abolitionists in the years to come.

THOMAS PAINE, KING GEORGE III, AND THE MARQUIS DE LAFAYETTE

The contributions of Thomas Paine, King George III, and the Marquis de Lafayette to the American Revolution are as follows:

- Thomas Paine, often described as the Father of the American Revolution, wrote *Common Sense*, a pro-independence pamphlet published in 1776. It used a new style of political writing to promote the American Revolution and democratic government and denounce British tyranny. *Common Sense* became very popular, serving as a rallying point for American revolutionaries.
- King George III was the king of Great Britain during the American Revolution, and was responsible for waging war against the colonies. He was criticized heavily in the Declaration of Independence.
- The Marquis de Lafayette was a French military general who served during the American Revolution under the command of George Washington. He played an important role in the siege at Yorktown, where he contained British forces long enough for reinforcements to arrive. The British were defeated, which ended the war.

PATRICK HENRY

Patrick Henry was a lawyer, orator, and politician who argued passionately over matters of liberty and the role of government as it involved the affairs of men. After winning a seat on the Virginia House of Burgesses in 1765, Henry joined in on the debate over the Stamp Act. Although the bill passed, Henry issued his own "Resolves." The Stamp Act Resolves outlined the unfair nature of being taxed by legislatures without due representation. He is often remembered for his now famous "Give me liberty or give me death" speech given to the Second Virginia Convention in 1775, which stirred many towards the idea of complete independence from Britain. Although he was invited to be a delegate at the 1787 Constitutional Convention, he refused because he did not agree with the Constitution as it was written. He was a staunch anti-federalist who supported limiting the power of the national government, with more power being apportioned to the states and desired a Bill of Rights.

GEORGE WASHINGTON

George Washington was nominated as the commander in chief of the Continental Army as well as elected as the first President of the United States. After the initial engagement of the Battle of Lexington and Concord, it was a primary concern of the Second Continental Congress to coordinate and unify the militias that had come to the defense of Boston. Washington had served as a major in the Virginia militia during the French and Indian War, and John Adams believed his experience and character would make him the best candidate for commander of the newly formed Continental Army. His steadfast leadership helped the American forces ultimately overcome the British forces despite numerous losses against the better equipped and funded troops. After the decisive victory in the Battle of Yorktown, the Revolutionary War came to its conclusion in 1781. In 1787, Washington was requested to attend the Constitutional Convention where his leadership was again noted and was pressured to run for President. He became the first President of the United States in 1789, despite never truly desiring the role.

FIRST CONTINENTAL CONGRESS

The goal of the First Continental Congress was to achieve a peaceful agreement with Britain. Made up of delegates from 12 of the 13 colonies, the Congress affirmed loyalty to Britain and the power of Parliament to dictate foreign affairs in the colonies. However, they demanded that the **Intolerable Acts** be repealed, and instituted a trade embargo with Britain until this came to pass.

In response, George III of England declared that the American colonies must submit or face military action. The British sought to end assemblies that opposed their policies. These assemblies gathered weapons and began to form militias. On April 19, 1775, the British military was ordered to disperse a meeting of the Massachusetts Assembly. A battle ensued on Lexington Common as the armed colonists resisted. The resulting battles became the **Battle of Lexington and Concord**—the first battles of the **American Revolution**.

SIGNIFICANCE OF THE SECOND CONTINENTAL CONGRESS

The Second Continental Congress met in Philadelphia on May 10, 1775, a month after Lexington and Concord. Their discussions centered on the defense of the American colonies and how to conduct the growing war, as well as local government. The delegates also discussed declaring independence from Britain, with many members in favor of this drastic move. They established an army, and on June 15, named **George Washington** as its commander in chief. By 1776, it was obvious that there was no turning back from full-scale war with Britain. The colonial delegates of the Continental Congress signed the **Declaration of Independence** on July 4, 1776.

> **Review Video: The First and Second Continental Congress**
> Visit mometrix.com/academy and enter code: 835211

ORIGINS AND BASIC IDEAS OF THE DECLARATION OF INDEPENDENCE

Penned by Thomas Jefferson and signed on July 4, 1776, the **Declaration of Independence** stated that King George III had violated the rights of the colonists and was establishing a tyrannical reign over them. Many of Jefferson's ideas of natural rights and property rights were shaped by 17th-century philosopher **John Locke**. Jefferson asserted all people's rights to "life, liberty and the pursuit of happiness." Locke's comparable idea asserted "life, liberty, and private property." Both felt that the purpose of government was to protect the rights of the people, and that individual rights were more important than individuals' obligations to the state.

BATTLES OF THE REVOLUTIONARY WAR

The following are five major battles of the Revolutionary War and their significance:

- The **Battle of Lexington and Concord** (April 1775) is considered the first engagement of the Revolutionary War.
- The **Battle of Bunker Hill** (June 1775) was one of the bloodiest of the entire war. Although American troops withdrew, about half of the British army was lost. The colonists proved they could stand against professional British soldiers. In August, Britain declared that the American colonies were officially in a state of rebellion.
- The first colonial victory occurred in Trenton, New Jersey, when Washington and his troops **crossed the Delaware River** on Christmas Day, 1776, for a December 26 surprise attack on British and Hessian troops.
- The **Battle of Saratoga** effectively ended a plan to separate the New England colonies from their Southern counterparts. The surrender of British general John Burgoyne led to France joining the war as allies of the Americans and is generally considered a turning point of the war.
- On October 19, 1781, General Cornwallis surrendered after a defeat in the **Battle of Yorktown**, ending the Revolutionary War.

> **Review Video: The American Revolutionary War**
> Visit mometrix.com/academy and enter code: 935282

SIGNIFICANCE OF THE TREATY OF PARIS

The Treaty of Paris was signed on September 3, 1783, bringing an official end to the Revolutionary War. In this document, Britain officially recognized the United States of America as an **independent nation**. The treaty established the Mississippi River as the country's western border. The treaty also restored Florida to Spain, while France reclaimed African and Caribbean colonies seized by the British in 1763. On November 25, 1783, the last British troops departed from the newly born United States of America.

SIGNIFICANCE OF THE ARTICLES OF CONFEDERATION

A precursor to the Constitution, the **Articles of Confederation** represented the first attempt of the newly independent colonies to establish the basics of government. The Continental Congress approved the Articles on November 15, 1777. They went into effect on March 1, 1781, following ratification by the thirteen states. The articles prevented a central government from gaining too much power, instead giving power to a **congressional body** made up of **delegates** from all thirteen states. However, the individual states retained final authority.

Without a strong central **executive**, though, this weak alliance among the new states proved ineffective in settling disputes or enforcing laws. The idea of a weak central government needed to be revised. Recognition of these weaknesses eventually led to the drafting of a new document, the **Constitution**.

INITIAL PROPOSITION AND DRAFT OF THE CONSTITUTION

Delegates from twelve of the thirteen states (Rhode Island was not represented) met in Philadelphia in May of 1787, initially intending to revise the Articles of Confederation. However, it quickly became apparent that a simple revision would not provide the workable governmental structure the newly formed country needed. After vowing to keep all the proceedings secret until the final document was completed, the delegates set out to draft what would eventually become the **Constitution of the United States of America**. By keeping the negotiations secret, the delegates

were able to present a completed document to the country for ratification, rather than having every small detail hammered out by the general public.

Review Video: Who Drafted the Constitution?
Visit mometrix.com/academy and enter code: 662451

GENERAL STRUCTURE OF GOVERNMENT PROPOSED BY THE DELEGATES

The delegates agreed that the new nation required a **strong central government** but that its overall power should be **limited**. The various branches of the government should have **balanced power**, so that no one group could control the others. Final power belonged to the **citizens** who voted officials into office based on who would provide the best representation.

THE EARLY REPUBLIC AND AGE OF JACKSON

SIGNIFICANCE OF THE VIRGINIA PLAN, THE NEW JERSEY PLAN, AND THE GREAT COMPROMISE

Disagreement immediately occurred between delegates from large states and those from smaller states. James Madison and Edmund Randolph (the governor of Virginia) felt that representation in Congress should be based on state population. This was the **Virginia Plan**. The **New Jersey Plan**, presented by William Paterson from New Jersey, proposed that each state should have equal representation. Finally, Roger Sherman from Connecticut formulated the **Connecticut Compromise**, also called the Great Compromise. The result was the familiar structure we have today. Each state has the equal representation of two Senators in the Senate, with the number of representatives in the House of Representatives based on population. This is called a **bicameral congress**. Both houses may draft bills, but financial matters must originate in the House of Representatives.

EFFECTS OF THE THREE-FIFTHS COMPROMISE AND THE NUMBER OF REPRESENTATIVES FOR EACH STATE

During debate on the US Constitution, a disagreement arose between the Northern and Southern states involving how **slaves** should be counted when determining a state's quota of representatives. In the South, large numbers of slaves were commonly used to run plantations. Delegates wanted slaves to be counted to determine the number of representatives but not counted to determine the amount of taxes the states would pay. The Northern states wanted exactly the opposite arrangement. The final decision was to count three-fifths of the slave population both for tax purposes and to determine representation. This was called the **Three-fifths Compromise**.

PROVISIONS OF THE COMMERCE COMPROMISE

The Commerce Compromise also resulted from a North/South disagreement. In the North, the economy was centered on **industry and trade**. The Southern economy was largely **agricultural**. The Northern states wanted to give the new government the ability to regulate exports as well as trade between the states. The South opposed this plan. Another compromise was in order. In the end, Congress received regulatory power over all trade, including the ability to collect **tariffs** on exported goods. In the South, this raised another red flag regarding the slave trade, as they were concerned about the effect on their economy if tariffs were levied on slaves. The final agreement allowed importing slaves to continue for twenty years without government intervention. Import taxes on slaves were limited, and after the year 1808, Congress could decide whether to allow continued imports of slaves.

OBJECTIONS AGAINST THE CONSTITUTION

Once the Constitution was drafted, it was presented for approval by the states. Nine states needed to approve the document for it to become official. However, debate and discussion continued. Major **concerns** included:

- There was nobill of rights to protect individual freedoms.
- States felt too much power was being handed over to the central government.
- Voters wanted more control over their elected representatives.

Discussion about necessary changes to the Constitution was divided into two camps: Federalists and Anti-Federalists. **Federalists** wanted a strong central government. **Anti-Federalists** wanted to prevent a tyrannical government from developing if a central government held too much power.

BEGINNING OF THE FEDERALIST PERIOD AND THE JUDICIARY ACT OF 1789

After the ratification of the Constitution, **George Washington** was inaugurated as the first **president** in New York City. He immediately went outside the Constitution to form the first **Cabinet**: Thomas Jefferson, Secretary of State; Alexander Hamilton, Secretary of the Treasury; Henry Knox, Secretary of War; Edmund Randolph, Attorney General; and Samuel Osgood, Postmaster General. With the **Judiciary Act of 1789**, it was decided that there would be six justices and one chief justice on the Supreme Court. This act also established the federal court system and the policy of judicial review, whereby federal courts made sure that state courts and laws did not violate the Constitution. This policy was inspired by the case **Chisholm v. Georgia**, in which the Supreme Court ruled that a citizen of South Carolina could sue the state of Georgia and that the case must be heard in a Georgia state court.

HAMILTON'S FUNDING AND ECONOMIC PLAN FOR THE FINANCIAL SYSTEM

The United States was born with $80 million in debt. **Alexander Hamilton**, however, was not terribly concerned by this; on the contrary, he encouraged **credit** as a means of financing the rapid capital improvements that would aid economic expansion. Hamilton introduced a **funding process**, whereby the government would buy back government bonds at full price in order to place money into the economy. Unfortunately, word of this plan leaked to some speculators, who bought the bonds at reduced rates and made huge profits. This led to accusations of a conspiracy. Another aspect of Hamilton's economic plan was for the federal government to **assume state debts**. This was done in part to tie state governments to the national government.

CUSTOM DUTIES, EXCISE TAXES, AND FEDERAL BANKS

In order to pay off the national debt, Hamilton promoted the **Revenue Act of 1789**, which was ostensibly a tax on imports, though it amounted to very little. Hamilton hoped to appease American industry with this measure without alienating foreign interests. The **Whiskey Tax**, instituted in 1791, was another attempt to generate revenue. This tax was wildly unpopular, however, and Washington was forced to call in several state militias to deal with various uprisings. At this time, Hamilton was also trying to establish a national bank, based upon the Bank of England. The **Bank of America** was established with $10 million in capital and aimed to repay foreign debts, provide a uniform national currency, aid in the collection of taxes, make loans, and act as a federal depository.

PROVISIONS OF THE COMMERCE COMPROMISE

The Commerce Compromise also resulted from a North/South disagreement. In the North, the economy was centered on **industry and trade**. The Southern economy was largely **agricultural**. The Northern states wanted to give the new government the ability to regulate exports as well as trade between the states. The South opposed this plan. Another compromise was in order. In the end, Congress received regulatory power over all trade, including the ability to collect **tariffs** on exported goods. In the South, this raised another red flag regarding the slave trade, as they were concerned about the effect on their economy if tariffs were levied on slaves. The final agreement allowed importing slaves to continue for twenty years without government intervention. Import taxes on slaves were limited, and after the year 1808, Congress could decide whether to allow continued imports of slaves.

DEVELOPMENT OF POLITICAL PARTIES

George Washington was adamantly against the establishment of political parties, based on the abuses perpetrated by such parties in Britain. However, political parties developed in US politics almost from the beginning. Major parties throughout US History have included:

- Federalists and Democratic-Republicans—formed in the late 1700s and disagreed on the balance of power between national and state government.
- Democrats and Whigs—developed before the Civil War, based on disagreements about various issues such as slavery.
- Democrats and Republicans—developed after the Civil War, with issues centering on the treatment of the post-war South.
- While third parties sometimes enter the picture in US politics, the government is basically a two-party system, dominated by the Democrats and Republicans.

CAUSES AND RESULT OF THE WAR OF 1812

The War of 1812 grew out of the continuing tension between France and Great Britain. Napoleon continued striving to conquer Britain, while the US continued trade with both countries but favored France and the French colonies. Because of what Britain saw as an alliance between America and France, they determined to bring an end to trade between the two nations.

With the British preventing US trade with the French and the French preventing trade with the British, James Madison's presidency introduced acts to **regulate international trade**. If either Britain or France removed their restrictions, America would not trade with the other country. Napoleon acted first, and Madison prohibited trade with England. England saw this as the US formally siding with the French, and war ensued in 1812.

The **War of 1812** has been called the **Second American Revolution**. It established the superiority of the US naval forces and reestablished US independence from Britain and Europe.

The British had two major objections to America's continued trade with France. First, they saw the US as helping France's war effort by providing supplies and goods. Second, the United States had grown into a competitor, taking trade and money away from British ships and tradesmen. In its attempts to end American trade with France, the British put into effect the **Orders in Council**, which made any and all French-owned ports off-limits to American ships. They also began to seize American ships and conscript their crews.

> **Review Video: Overview of the War of 1812**
> Visit mometrix.com/academy and enter code: 507716
>
> **Review Video: Opinions About the War of 1812**
> Visit mometrix.com/academy and enter code: 274558

WASHINGTON'S ACCOMPLISHMENTS AND FAREWELL ADDRESS

In 1796, Washington decided he was too tired to continue as president. In his famous Farewell Address, he implored the United States to avoid three things: permanent alliances; political factions; and sectionalism. Washington felt that the nation could only be successful if people placed the nation ahead of their own region. For his own part, Washington made some significant improvements during his presidency. He avoided war at a time when the nation was vulnerable. He also avoided political alliances and promoted the national government without alienating great numbers of people. Washington oversaw Hamilton's creation of the economic system and guided expansion to the West (as well as the creation of three new states: Vermont, Kentucky, and Tennessee).

JAMES MONROE

In the election of 1816, the Democrat-Republican James Monroe defeated the last Federalist candidate, Rufus King, by a landslide. The Federalist opposition to the War of 1812 doomed the party to extinction. Monroe's early term was not without its problems, however. A mild depression caused by over-speculation on western lands led to the Panic of 1819, and began a 20-year boom-bust cycle. These problems were exacerbated by the Second Bank of the United States; the Bank's pressure on the so-called "wildcat" banks to foreclose on properties, as well as the unwillingness of the Bank to loan money, made it very unpopular. The nationalism generated by the War of 1812 was damaged by these economic travails.

In 1823, President James Monroe formulated a foreign policy which is known today as the Monroe Doctrine. In his annual address to Congress, Monroe indicated that the Old World (namely Europe) and the New World (namely the United States) were distinct entities with distinct systems, and should therefore exist as separate spheres. His statement included four main points:

- the United States would not participate in conflicts within or between European nations
- the United States officially recognized and would not interfere with existing colonies in the New World
- the Western Hemisphere was off limits for future colonization
- any endeavor by a European power to influence any nation in the Western Hemisphere would be considered a hostile act against the United States.

Though the Monroe Doctrine was militarily unsustainable at the time of its formulation, as the U.S. emerged as a global power in the 1870's, the Monroe Doctrine came to be viewed as a geopolitical definition of the country's sphere of influence as the entire Western Hemisphere.

MONROE DOCTRINE

The Monroe Doctrine was a statement of foreign policy created by President James Monroe and Secretary of State John Quincy Adams. The document stated that Europe should not interfere in affairs within the United States or with the creation of other countries in the Western Hemisphere. Likewise, the United States would not get involved in European matters. In 1823, when the doctrine was announced, the United States was facing Russian claims to the Northwest Coast, and governments in Latin America wanted independence from Spain. The doctrine reflected growing nationalism and a decreased interest in international affairs. President Polk revived the doctrine in 1845, and it continued to be important ideologically into the next century.

ANDREW JACKSON

Andrew Jackson is often seen as a symbol of the rising power of the New West, or as an embodiment of the "rags to riches" fable. He spent much of his presidency trying to promote the idea of nationalism at a time when most of the country was ardently sectionalist. During his presidency, he dominated Congress, vetoing more legislation than all of the previous presidents combined. He was also famous for his so-called "Kitchen Cabinet," a group of close advisers without official positions. Many of these men later received formal appointments, including as Secretary of State (Martin van Buren), Postmaster General (Amos Kendall), and Secretary of the Treasury (Roger B. Taney). The election of 1828 is considered the first modern campaign in American politics. Andrew Jackson had the first campaign manager, Amos Kendall, and produced buttons, posters, and slogans to support his candidacy. These men—Jackson, Kendall, John C. Calhoun, and Martin van Buren—formed the beginning of the Democratic party. Meanwhile, the incumbent John Quincy Adams ran a very formal campaign, with little of the "flesh-pressing" of Jackson. Adams tried to discredit Jackson as an adulterer and bigamist because Jackson's wife had not been officially divorced at the time of their marriage. When his wife died during the campaign, however, the popular sentiment returned to Jackson, and he won the election by a considerable margin. Jackson's inauguration was an over-crowded, chaotic affair; the president suffered three cracked ribs during the festivities.

> **Review Video: Andrew Jackson's Presidency**
> Visit mometrix.com/academy and enter code: 667792

INDIAN REMOVAL ACT OF 1830 AND THE TREATY OF NEW ECHOTA

The Indian Removal Act of 1830 gave the new American government power to form treaties with Native Americans. In theory, America would claim land east of the Mississippi in exchange for land west of the Mississippi, to which the natives would relocate voluntarily. In practice, many tribal leaders were forced into signing the treaties, and relocation at times occurred by force.

The **Treaty of New Echota** in 1835 was supposedly a treaty between the US government and Cherokee tribes in Georgia. However, the treaty was not signed by tribal leaders but rather by a small portion of the represented people. The leaders protested and refused to leave, but President Martin Van Buren enforced the treaty by sending soldiers. During their forced relocation, more than 4,000 Cherokee Indians died on what became known as the **Trail of Tears**.

> **Review Video: Indian Removal Act**
> Visit mometrix.com/academy and enter code: 666738

WORCESTER V. GEORGIA

In 1830, Jackson set a precedent by vetoing the funding of a road that was to be entirely within one state (Kentucky). Many believed that Jackson vetoed this bill to spite Henry Clay, but the move had some positive political consequences as well: the Southerners appreciated the idea that states should tend to their own business, and northerners liked it because the road would have given people easier access to the West. Jackson's attempts at relocating Native Americans were less successful. The passage of the Indian Resettlement Act of 1830 was the first attempt by the national government to force migration. In the case of Worcester v. Georgia (1832), the Supreme Court ruled against those who sought to grab Native lands. John Marshall asserted that the Cherokee nation was sovereign, but a ward of the US. Despite Marshall's assertion of Native American rights, Jackson supported the slow and steady conquest of land in the South and West.

PHILADELPHIA CONVENTION OF 1787

The Philadelphia Convention is also known as the Constitutional Convention. Arguments for and against ratification of the constitution were presented at the convention by the Federalists and anti-Federalists, respectively. The Federalists supported ratification because they felt that the

Constitution would allow the people to protect their freedom and rights. The anti-Federalists argued that the Constitution was too centralizing—that is, put too much power in the hands of the federal government--and would destroy the liberty so hard won in the American Revolution. The Federalists were very well organized and had strong political support. The anti-Federalists were a much more loosely formed group. A lively newspaper debate occurred before each state voted on ratification.

LOUISIANA PURCHASE

In 1803 the United States acquired the Louisiana Territory from France. The U.S. government, which was led by President Thomas Jefferson, purchased the territory from Napoleon Bonaparte, ruler of France, for $15 million. The land area of the United States more than doubled with the purchase, which included all of the land from the Mississippi River to the Rocky Mountains. This land was full of fertile plains and vital waterways, and later became all or part of 13 states: Louisiana, Missouri, Arkansas, Iowa, Minnesota, Kansas, Nebraska, Colorado, North Dakota, South Dakota, Montana, Wyoming, and Oklahoma.

PHYSICAL CHARACTERISTICS COMPARED TO ORIGINAL 13 COLONIES

The original 13 states were located along the East Coast of North America. The land was close to water. Proximity to water is vital to settlement for many reasons. Goods can be brought in and sent out, and water is needed to successfully grow crops. Almost all of the land gained from the Louisiana Purchase was inland. Only the southern tip of Louisiana is located on water. Most of the land is flat prairie, much of it good farmland. After the acquisition of this land, surveyors were sent to bring back information about the quality of the land to those living in the East who were interested in moving West.

WESTWARD EXPANSION
NORTHWEST ORDINANCE

The Northwest Ordinance is considered one of the most important aspects of the Articles of Confederation and has had a lasting impact. Passed in 1787, the Northwest Ordinance made provisions for setting up governments in the western territories. With such governments, these territories eventually could join the Union and be equal with the original 13 states. The Northwest Ordinance is the reason that the United States was able to grow. Because of the ordinance, the United States expanded westward by the creation of new states instead of expanding the existing ones. The Northwest Territories referenced in the document included parts of Illinois, Ohio, Indiana, Michigan, Wisconsin, and parts of Minnesota. According to the ordinance, after 5,000 adult males moved into a territory, they could form a general assembly and send a nonvoting delegate to Congress. When 60,000 people moved into a territory, they could draft and submit a constitution. If approved, the territory could become a state. The first state created from a territory was Ohio, in 1803.

WESTWARD EXPANSION

America's westward expansion led to conflict and violent confrontations with Native Americans such as the Battle of Little Bighorn. In 1876, the American government ordered all Indians to relocate to reservations. Lack of compliance led to the Dawes Act in 1887, which ordered assimilation rather than separation. This act remained in effect until 1934. Reformers also forced Indian children to attend Indian Boarding Schools, where they were not allowed to speak their native language and were forced to accept Christianity. Children were often abused in these schools, and were indoctrinated to abandon their identity as Native Americans.

In 1890, the massacre at Wounded Knee, accompanied by Geronimo's surrender, led the Native Americans to work to preserve their culture rather than fight for their lands.

MANIFEST DESTINY

Manifest Destiny was the popular belief in the 1840s that the United States was destined to cover the entire area from the Atlantic Ocean to the Pacific Ocean. Manifest Destiny led to the acquisition of the Oregon Territory from Britain during the presidency of James Polk in the 1840s. After the Mexican War of 1848, a large swath of southwest territory was gained as well. This included the land of California, Nevada, and Utah, and parts of Arizona, Colorado, New Mexico, and Wyoming.

> **Review Video: What is the Manifest Destiny?**
> Visit mometrix.com/academy and enter code: 957409

LOUISIANA PURCHASE

The area acquired by the Louisiana Purchase included the present states of Arkansas, Missouri, Iowa, Oklahoma, Kansas, and Nebraska. Parts of Minnesota, North Dakota, South Dakota, New Mexico, Montana, Wyoming, Colorado, and Louisiana were included as well. The Louisiana Purchase doubled the area of the United States at the time. The acquired area is marked by the dark border in the map below.

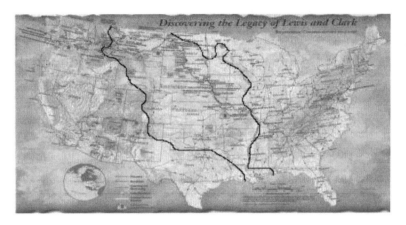

TERRITORIES AND TERRITORIAL ACQUISITIONS

The following were major territories or territorial acquisitions in the late 1700s and early 1800s:

- The Northwest Territory was established in 1787. It included all United States land west of Pennsylvania and northwest of the Ohio River, covering the present-day states of Ohio, Indiana, Illinois, Michigan, Wisconsin, and Minnesota. The United States acquired the Northwest Territory from Britain through the Treaty of Paris.
- The Southwest Territory was established in 1790. When it was admitted to the United States, it became the present-day state of Tennessee and part of the Mississippi Territory. The Southwest Territory was originally part of South Carolina, but was eventually ceded to the United States government.
- The Michigan Territory was established in 1805. It eventually became the present-day state of Michigan. The British government ceded the Michigan Territory to the United States government in 1783.
- The Louisiana Purchase was a territorial acquisition in which the United States purchased a large area of land from France in 1803. The area of land included 14 present-day states.

US-MEXICAN WAR

The immediate causes of the Mexican War were the American annexation of Texas, disputes over the Southern border of Texas and the large amount of money owed to the United States by Mexico. Moreover, it was well known that the Mexicans held the US in contempt, considering them greedy land-grabbers. Polk sent an emissary to buy Texas, California, and some Mexican territory for $30 million; he was refused. Zachary Taylor then led an American expedition into a disputed area of Texas where some of them were killed. Polk was able to use these deaths as a rationale for war, despite considerable opposition in Congress. Overall, the Democrats supported the war, while the Whigs, led in part by Abraham Lincoln, were opposed.

> **Review Video: When was the Mexican-American War?**
> Visit mometrix.com/academy and enter code: 271216

CIVIL WAR ERA

TARIFF POLICIES AND THE CIVIL WAR

Tariffs are taxes that a government levies on imported goods in order to raise funds. Because tariffs are added to foreign-made products, those products become more expensive than American-made goods. The Northern and Southern states had very different attitudes toward tariffs. Northern businessmen generally favored tariffs because they gave them an advantage over foreign companies. Southerners, on the other hand, sold most of their cotton to foreign buyers in exchange for foreign credit they could use to purchase foreign goods. But, this meant they had to buy foreign products, which cost more than domestic ones. The fact that these products were more expensive put the South at a disadvantage. Northerners and Southerners wanted the federal government to do opposing things with respect to tariffs.

SOUTHERN CROPS DURING THE 1800S

The most important crops grown in the South during the 1800s were cotton and tobacco. Rice, indigo, and sugar were other major cash crops for the South during this period. The South relied on agriculture much more than did the Northern states. Growing and harvesting crops requires much manpower. For this reason, Southern whites depended on slaves. This economic dependence allowed slavery to become an integral part of Southern life, which, in turn, led to sharp differences between the North and South, and, eventually, the Civil War.

ECONOMIC REASONS FOR GROWTH OF THE SLAVE TRADE

Economic reasons were a major factor in the growth of the slave trade in the South before the Civil War. Plantation owners needed abundant cheap labor in order to make money growing rice, cotton, sugar, tobacco and other products they exported abroad. Slaves were basically free labor, though owners did need to feed and clothe them. Plantation owners would buy more slaves in order to grow more crops to make more money, Slavery was basically a way for plantation owners to exploit a source of labor for their own profit, but it became entrenched in the economy of the South.

POLITICAL EFFECTS OF SLAVERY

Advocates of states' rights believed that the powers of the individual state were paramount to those of the federal government. The issue of each state, as opposed to the federal government, having sovereign authority over its citizens led to the secession of the South, which, in turn, led to the Civil War. Southerners believed they had a right to make decisions for themselves regarding slavery and taxes, among other issues. They did not think the federal government could tell them what to do. Because Southerners believed that the power of the Union rested in each state making decisions for itself based on its self-interest, states in the South began to secede from the Union.

THE CIVIL WAR

The Civil War was fought for a number of reasons, but the most important of these was the controversy about slavery. The issue of slavery touched on moral, economic, and political themes. Also, the differing geography of the North and South had caused the latter to develop an economy that they felt could only survive through slavery. The Civil War also sprang from the ongoing debate over states' rights; many in the South felt that states should have the power to nullify federal regulations and believed that the North had too much representation in Congress; and, indeed, the North had received much more federal aid for infrastructure. Finally, there was a general difference in culture between the North and South; the North was more of a dynamic and democratic society, while the South was more of a static oligarchy.

> **Review Video: Overview of the Civil War**
> Visit mometrix.com/academy and enter code: 239557

JOHN QUINCY ADAMS

All the major candidates in the 1824 election were Democrat-Republicans. Although Andrew Jackson received more electoral votes than John Quincy Adams, he did not win a majority, and Adams (with the help of Henry Clay) won the run-off in the House of Representatives. Adams was a fierce nationalist at a time when many in the country were sectionalist. Although his initiatives for a national university and public funding for the arts were well-meaning, Adams was still believed to be out of touch with the common man. He further alienated the middle and lower classes with the Tariff of 1828, known in the South as the "Tariff of Abominations." The South was already on shaky economic ground and the tariff became a scapegoat for its troubles. John C. Calhoun was an especially ardent Southern voice; he futilely proposed that states should have the ability to nullify federal regulations.

> **Review Video: John Quincy Adams as President**
> Visit mometrix.com/academy and enter code: 797549

EFFECTS OF LINCOLN'S ELECTION

In the election of 1860, Abraham Lincoln defeated three other challengers. Lincoln's platform was anti-slavery, though he vowed to leave it intact where it already existed. He also promised full rights to immigrants, the completion of a Pacific Railroad, free homesteads, and a protective tariff. After the election, South Carolina seceded, followed by the rest of the Deep South (Mississippi, Alabama, Georgia, Louisiana, Florida and Texas). These states established the Confederate States of America, with its capital in Montgomery, Alabama. The president of the CSA was Jefferson Davis. Outgoing US President Buchanan claimed that he had no constitutional authority to stop the secession, but upon entering office Lincoln attempted to maintain control of all Southern forts. This led to the firing on Ft. Sumter (SC) by the Confederates. As Lincoln called for aid, the Upper South (Virginia, Arkansas, North Carolina and Tennessee) seceded as well, and the CSA made Richmond, Virginia its new capital.

ROBERT E. LEE

Robert E. Lee was the commander of the Confederate Army of Northern Virginia during the Civil War. In 1861, President Lincoln offered Lee command of the Union Army, but Lee declined because his home state, Virginia, was threatening to secede from the Union. When the Confederacy was established, Lee became a senior military advisor to President Jefferson Davis. General Lee led many great battles but was unable to invade the North. He surrendered at Appomattox Courthouse in 1865, which marked the beginning of the end for the South. Only two months later, the last of the Confederate Armies surrendered.

WILLIAM H. CARNEY

Willam H. Carney served as a member of the 54th Massachusetts Infantry Regiment in 1863—an all-black unit besides some senior leaders. Born a freeman after his father had escaped slavery and purchased his family's freedom, Carney deeply believed it was necessary for him to join the Union forces in order to, "…best serve my God serving my country and my oppressed brothers." During the Battle of Fort Wagner, Carney displayed incredible bravery as he carried the flag after his color sergeant went down in the skirmish. Despite being shot four times, Carney managed to carry the flag to the fort and eventually back to the ranks of the 54th where he proclaimed, "Boys, the old flag never touched the ground!" Carney was the first African American soldier to receive the Medal of Honor when it was awarded to him in 1900.

PHILLIP BAZAAR

Philip Bazaar served as an ordinary seaman aboard the *U.S.S. Santiago de Cuba* during the US Civil War. He was an immigrant from Chile who had made his way to Massachusetts before finding work at the Union Navy. During the second assault on Fort Fisher in 1864, Bazaar and 5 other crew members carried dispatches to Major General Alfred Terry on land while taking heavy fire from the confederate forces. For his valor, Philip and the rest of his crew were awarded the US Navy Medal of Honor. Bazaar was the first South American recipient of this award.

STATES' RIGHTS AND THE CIVIL WAR

Advocates of states' rights believed that the powers of the individual state were equal to or greater than those of the federal government. The issue of each state, as opposed to the federal government, having sovereign authority over its citizens led to the secession of the South, which, in turn, led to the Civil War. Southerners believed they had a right to make decisions for themselves regarding slavery and taxes, among other issues. They did not think the federal government was constitutionally authorized to tell them what to do. Because Southerners believed that the power of the Union rested in each state making decisions for itself based on its self-interest, states in the South began to secede from the Union.

IMPORTANT BATTLES AND PEOPLE OF THE CIVIL WAR

- The **Battle of Fort Sumter** (1861) was the first battle of the American Civil War. Confederate troops bombarded Fort Sumter near Charleston, South Carolina, and forced the Union troops to abandon it.
- The **Battle of Gettysburg** (1863) was a major battle during the American Civil War. It resulted in the largest number of casualties, and saw the tide turn in favor of the North.
- The **Battle of Appomattox Court House** (1865) was one of the final battles of the America Civil War, and ended with General Robert E. Lee surrendering to General Ulysses S. Grant.
- **General Robert E. Lee** was the commander of the Army of Northern Virginia during the American Civil War, and was eventually promoted to general-in-chief of the Confederate forces.
- **General Ulysses S. Grant** was the commander of all Union forces during the American Civil War. He was later elected the 18th President of the United States.
- The **Battle of Vicksburg** (1863) was a 47-day siege that resulted in a decisive victory for Grant and the Union, as well as crippled the supply line of the Confederacy. Vicksburg was a valuable port along the Mississippi River and gaining control of it was part of the Union's Anaconda Plan to cut off the Confederate Army's outside trade.

BATTLE OF ANTIETAM AND THE EMANCIPATION PROCLAMATION

At the Battle of Antietam (MD) in September of 1862, the Confederate General Robert E. Lee went on the offensive, hoping to bring Maryland into the Confederacy, sever the channels between

Washington, DC and the North, and attract the recognition of the European powers. This was the bloodiest battle of the Civil War and ended in a draw. It was after this battle that Lincoln issued his famous Emancipation Proclamation. This document freed the slaves in any area that was taken by the Union, or in areas from which slaves could enter the Union. It did not, however, free slaves in the Border States, because Lincoln wanted to maintain loyalty to the Union in these areas. The aims of the Emancipation Proclamation were three: to keep the British from assisting the South, to motivate the Northern troops and to effect a positive moral change.

> **Review Video: The Civil War: The Emancipation Proclamation**
> Visit mometrix.com/academy and enter code: 181778

ABRAHAM LINCOLN

Abraham Lincoln, the 16th President of the United States, is best known for leading the country through the Civil War. Lincoln began his political career in 1832 at the age 23 when he ran for the Illinois General Assembly. He lost that election but on his second attempt two years later, he was elected. In 1846, Lincoln was elected to a single term in the U.S. House of Representatives. After serving his two-year term, he returned to Springfield to practice law. In the presidential race of 1860, Lincoln defeated Stephen Douglas, John Breckinridge, and John Bell to become the 16th President of the United States. By February of 1861, seven states had seceded from the Union and formed the Confederate States of America.

BEGINNING OF THE CIVIL WAR

On April 12, 1861, Confederate forces fired on Union troops at Fort Sumter, effectively beginning the Civil War. Lincoln took several immediate actions to quell the rebellion: expanding his war powers, imposing a blockade on Confederate shipping ports, disbursing funds without the approval of Congress, and suspending habeas corpus to allow the arrest and imprisonment of thousands of suspected Confederate sympathizers without trials.

EMANCIPATION PROCLAMATION

In January of 1863, more than a year and a half into the Civil War, Lincoln signed a presidential proclamation declaring that all slaves in the states still in rebellion against the Union were thereby freed. Over the course of the next several years, all states were encouraged or coerced into prohibiting human slavery as a practice.

GETTYSBURG ADDRESS

The Gettysburg Address was a speech that President Abraham Lincoln delivered in Gettysburg, Pennsylvania, during the Civil War. The speech was given to dedicate a national cemetery on the grounds of the Battle of Gettysburg. President Lincoln's speech was a comment on the ideals of democracy: liberty and freedom for all. He felt that these ideals were being threatened by the Civil War. He reminded the country that it was founded on the precept that all men are created equal and that the country fought hard to have a government of the people, by the people, and for the people. He wanted the citizens to join together to preserve the ideals of democracy.

RECONSTRUCTION ERA

RECONSTRUCTION AND 13TH, 14TH, AND 15TH AMENDMENTS

Reconstruction was the period from 1865 to 1877, during which the South was under strict control of the U.S. government. In March, 1867, all state governments of the former Confederacy were terminated, and **military occupation** began. Military commanders called for constitutional conventions to reconstruct the state governments, to which delegates were to be elected by universal male suffrage. After a state government was in operation and the state had **ratified the**

14th Amendment, its representatives were admitted to Congress. Three constitutional amendments from 1865 to 1870, which tried to rectify the problems caused by slavery, became part of the Reconstruction effort. The **13th Amendment** declared slavery illegal. The **14th Amendment** made all persons born or naturalized in the country U.S. citizens, and forbade any state to interfere with their fundamental civil rights. The **15th Amendment** made it illegal to deny individuals the right to vote on the grounds of race. In his 1876 election campaign, President **Rutherford B. Hayes** promised to withdraw troops from the South, and did so in 1877.

> **Review Video: What is the 13th Amendment?**
> Visit mometrix.com/academy and enter code: 800185
>
> **Review Video: What is the 14th Amendment?**
> Visit mometrix.com/academy and enter code: 851325
>
> **Review Video: What is the 15th Amendment?**
> Visit mometrix.com/academy and enter code: 287199

IMPACT OF ELECTION OF AFRICAN AMERICANS FROM THE SOUTH

In the midst of the tumultuous Reconstruction Era, determining how the Southern states would rejoin the union and who would govern them became a paramount issue. Mississippi sought readmission into the US Congress and desperately needed to fill the vacant spots left by Albert Brown and Jefferson Davis. With the 15th Amendment on its way to ratification, the black members of the state legislation—now a significant percentage—insisted on filling one of the Senate seats with a black Republican. Hiram Revels, a minister and teacher, was elected as the first African American Senator of Mississippi in 1870. He championed education and civil rights for black Americans, fought against segregation and became a visible symbol of progress and hope for a better future following the end of the Civil War.

RECONSTRUCTION ERA

The Reconstruction Era in the United States began as the Civil War ended, and lasted until 1877. Its purpose was to address how the eleven states that had seceded from the Union would regain self-government and be reseated to Congress. It also focused on the Constitutional and legal status of both the former leaders of the Confederacy and the freed slaves. As Confederate states came back under the control of the U.S. Army, President Lincoln began setting up reconstructed governments in some of the states, and experimented with giving land to former slaves in others. After Lincoln's assassination in 1865, Democrat Andrew Johnson came to power and attempted to reign in the previous administration's plan for reconstruction. This action was met with fierce opposition in the Republican Congress and they rejected his terms, eventually voting to remove the civilian governments that had been established in the South and returned control to the U.S. Army. The period of Reconstruction ended at different times in different states, usually corresponding to the loss of Republican control in the state legislatures. With the Compromise of 1877, federal military intervention in the South finally ended.

> **Review Video: Reconstruction**
> Visit mometrix.com/academy and enter code: 790561

Geography and Culture

GEOGRAPHY
CONFEDERATE STATES OF AMERICA DURING THE CIVIL WAR

The area that made up the Confederate States of America during the Civil War included the states of Virginia, Georgia, North Carolina, South Carolina, Mississippi, Florida, Alabama, Louisiana, Texas, Arkansas, and Tennessee. These are all the states south of the thick line on the map below.

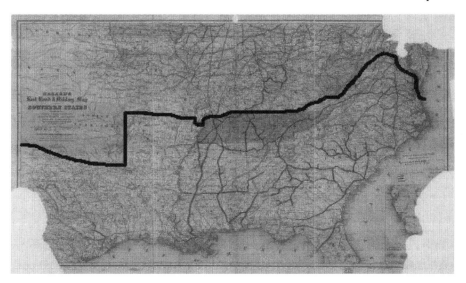

CLIMATE OF THE UNITED STATES

The U.S. has a vast distribution of geographical features, with mountain ranges in both east and west, stretches of fertile plains through the center, and large lakes and waterways. Many of these areas were shaped by glaciers, which also deposited highly fertile soil.

Because it is so large, the US experiences several varieties of climate, including continental climates with four seasons in median areas, tropical climates in the southern part of the US, and arctic climes in the far north. Human intervention has greatly influenced the productivity of agricultural regions, and many areas have been reshaped to accommodate easier, more economical transportation.

> **Review Video: What is Climate?**
> Visit mometrix.com/academy and enter code: 991320

ECONOMIC GEOGRAPHY OF THE UNITED STATES

As a current superpower, the United States has one of the most advanced economies in the world. Like Canada, the United States contains many deposits of natural resources. For instance, the North American realm has more coal reserves than any other. The spatial organization of regional agricultural production in the United States exists within the framework of a modified Von Thunen model, with the "megalopolis" of New England at its center, and belts of specialized activity extending westward. Though the manufacturing sector is less important in a postindustrial economy, this type of activity is still practiced in the United States, and tends to cluster around several urban-industrial nodes, especially within the Manufacturing Belt (located in the Northeast United States). Increased mechanization and advancements in technology have eliminated many "blue-collar" jobs in this region. Most laborers in the U.S. workforce are employed in quaternary economic activity. States offering noneconomic amenities (such as weather and proximity to urban centers and universities) have experienced higher levels of growth than other regions.

31

EXPANSION INTO TEXAS

In 1821, Mexico received its independence from Spain. Mexico sold Texan lands to Americans, yet these people were still required to live under Mexican civil law (for one thing, people had to convert to Catholicism). In 1832, however, Santa Anna led a coup in Mexico and decided to crack down on the Texans. This led to the Texas Revolution of 1836, in which Texan General William Travis' men were massacred by the forces of Santa Anna at the Alamo, in which both Davy Crockett and Jim Bowie were killed. After suffering some other defeats the Texans, led by Sam Houston, finally defeated Santa Anna at the Battle of San Jacinto in 1836 and he was forced below the Rio Grande. Nevertheless, Texas was not made part of the US, mainly because the issue of slavery was so contentious at the time. It would not be annexed and admitted into the Union until 1845.

U.S EXPANSION TO SALT LAKE CITY, OREGON, AND CALIFORNIA

The territory of Oregon became more important to the US government as fur-trapping became a lucrative industry. Oregon was also known to contain rich farmland. As for California, its natural bounty had been described by whalers since the 1820s. In the 1840s, whole families (including the ill-fated Donner party) began to migrate there. Around this time the Church of Jesus Christ of Latter-day Saints, otherwise known as the Mormon Church, was founded by Joseph Smith. Among the beliefs espoused by the Mormons were polygamy, communalism and the abolition of slavery. After Smith's death, the Mormons were led by Brigham Young and settled in what is now Salt Lake City. Meanwhile, in 1848 gold was discovered in a California stream, generating still more excitement over the economic potential of the West.

PANAMA CANAL

The Spanish-American War had demonstrated that the US needed a Latin American canal in order to become a major naval power. At that time, however, their hands were tied by the Clayton-Bulwer Treaty of 1850, which had stated that neither the US nor Britain would build a canal in Latin America without the other. Fortunately for the US, the British were distracted by the Boer War in South Africa and thus were willing to sign the Hay-Pauncefote Treaty in 1901, allowing the US to go it alone. Many in the US, including Roosevelt, wanted to build the canal in Nicaragua because it has a number of lakes that could be connected, and because it is mostly flat. Others lobbied for Panama, pointing out that a French contractor had already started work on a canal there and that Panama was narrower than Nicaragua.

Once Roosevelt finally secured the building supplies and the land to construct the Panama Canal, the brutal and dangerous work began. In order to prevent malaria the US paved streets, drained swamps, and built houses so that the workers would not have to sleep in tents. Nevertheless, the workdays were long and the pay was low. In the end, the canal cost about $400 million; it was finished in 1913, but did not open until the next year. Roosevelt's visit to Panama made him the first president to leave the US during his term. In 1920, a guilty Democratic Congress gave Colombia $25 million. At present, about 12,000 ships go through the canal every year and it takes about 8 hours to get from one end to the other.

CULTURE
CULTURES OF THE UNITED STATES

The United States supports a diverse culture, as it was formed from groups of native races as well as large numbers of immigrants. It functioned for a period under British rule. The United States broke from British rule via violent revolution. Agriculture, industries and technology all play a large part in the United States economy. The United States in general supports a high standard of living and a high level of development, and supports trade with countries throughout the world.

Immigrant Groups and their Reasons for Immigration

- **Pilgrims**–Fleeing religious persecution (1620-1630)
- **Puritans**–Fleeing from religious persecution (1620-1642)
- **Indentured Servants**–Seeking new opportunity and the chance at a better life (1642-1675)
- **Quakers**–Fleeing religious persecution (1675-1725)
- **Scottish, Irish, and English**–Series of crop failures and famines (1715-1775)
- **Dutch, Swedish, and German**–Seeking trade interests; fled economic and political hardship (1630-1783)
- **African slaves**–Kidnapped and involuntarily brought for forced labor (1619-1783)
- **Chinese**–Seeking economic opportunity from the California Gold Rush and crop failure (1839-1860)
- **Italians**–Seeking economic opportunity from rapid industrialization and urbanization (1880-1920)
- **Jews**–Fleeing religious persecution (1880-1920)

The Puritans

The Puritans established the colony of Massachusetts Bay in 1630. They hoped to purify the Church of England and then return to Europe with a new and improved religion. The Massachusetts Bay Puritans were more immediately successful than other fledgling colonies because they brought enough supplies, arrived in the springtime, and had good leadership (including John Winthrop). Puritans fished, cut timber for ships, and trapped fur. The local government was inextricably bound with the church; only church members were allowed to vote for the General Court (similar to the House of Burgesses), although everyone was required to pay taxes. The Puritans established a Bible Commonwealth that would last 50 years. During this time, Old Testament law was the law of the community.

There was more chance for social mobility in Massachusetts than in any other colony in America. This was mainly due to the diverse economy. As for religion, it dominated every area of an individual's life. The Puritan Church was known as the Congregational Church; at first, this was an exclusive group, but it gradually became easier to become a member. Indeed, by the mid-1600s religious fervor seemed to be waning in Massachusetts. A group called the Jeremiads warned the people that they were in danger of lapsing into atheism, but many people did not mind. Around this time, ministers began to offer half-way covenants, which gave church members partial privileges.

Non-English Immigrants

Most non-English immigrants were at one point or another marginalized in some way. Anti-Catholic & anti-immigrant parties rose up saying that they were taking away job opportunities. Irish, Italians, Jews, and Germans were often abused or the victim of hate crimes. They were often treated much like African Americans in many respects, including "separate but equal" style accommodations. Jews were forced into ghettos and slums alongside many other minorities. The Chinese Exclusion Act of 1882 was the first law passed that directly prevented an ethnic group from immigrating to the US and was upheld by the Supreme Court in an attempt to appease white workers who claimed they were losing their jobs to cheaper Chinese laborers.

Melting-Pot Culture

The influx of such a variety of cultures and ethnicities gave America the label of a "melting pot" because it was able to mix all of the uniqueness of so many cultures into a place where everyone could come and pursue better lives. However, to say America was a wholly inclusive land is far from the truth, as much of American tradition can be tied to trying to stamp out foreign identities or

force them to assimilate to the dominant majority. Despite the injustices so many immigrants faced, they endured the hardships of their time and developed bustling cultural centers and legacies that have withstood the test of time.

NEW ENGLAND COLONIES

The New England colonies were New Hampshire, Connecticut, Rhode Island and Massachusetts. These colonies were founded largely to escape **religious persecution** in England. The beliefs of the **Puritans**, who migrated to America in the 1600s, significantly influenced the development of these colonies. Situated in the northeast coastal areas of America, the New England colonies featured numerous harbors as well as dense forests. The soil, however, was rocky and had a very short growing season, so was not well suited for agriculture. The economy of New England during the colonial period centered around fishing, shipbuilding and trade along with some small farms and lumber mills. Although some groups congregated in small farms, life centered mainly in towns and cities where **merchants** largely controlled the trade economy. Coastal cities such as Boston grew and thrived.

> **Review Video: The Massachusetts Bay Colony**
> Visit mometrix.com/academy and enter code: 407058

MIDDLE OR MIDDLE ATLANTIC COLONIES

The Middle or Middle Atlantic Colonies were New York, New Jersey, Pennsylvania, and Delaware. Unlike the New England colonies, where most colonists were from England and Scotland, the Middle Colonies founders were from various countries, including the Netherlands and Sweden. Various factors led these colonists to America. More fertile than New England, the Middle Colonies became major producers of **crops**, including rye, oats, potatoes, wheat, and barley. Some particularly wealthy inhabitants owned large farms and/or businesses. Farmers, in general, were able to produce enough to have a surplus to sell. Tenant farmers also rented land from larger landowners.

SOUTHERN COLONIES

The Southern Colonies were Maryland, Virginia, North Carolina, South Carolina, and Georgia. Of the Southern Colonies, Virginia was the first permanent English colony and Georgia the last. The warm climate and rich soil of the south encouraged **agriculture**, and the growing season was long. As a result, economy in the south was based largely on labor-intensive **plantations**. Crops included tobacco, rice, and indigo, all of which became valuable cash crops. Most land in the south was controlled by wealthy plantation owners and farmers. Labor on the farms came in the form of indentured servants and African slaves. The first of these **African slaves** arrived in Virginia in 1619.

> **Review Video: Southern Colonies: An Overview**
> Visit mometrix.com/academy and enter code: 703830
>
> **Review Video: The English Colony of Virginia**
> Visit mometrix.com/academy and enter code: 537399

CONTRIBUTIONS OF WOMEN TO AMERICAN SOCIETY

For nearly a century of America's history, women were mostly viewed as insignificant or delicate and had no place or desire for roles outside of the home. When the Civil War began, women were able to break out of their traditional gender roles in mighty ways. Many women raised money for war efforts, served in militias and industry, supplied food for troops, or worked as nurses behind

combat lines. Many women worked with the Underground Railroad to aid runaway slaves and campaigned for women's suffrage. Through their efforts, many slaves were able to escape to freedom and Wyoming first allowed women to vote in 1869. However, women would have to continue lobbying for the national right to vote for decades to come.

ABOLITIONIST MOVEMENT

The abolitionist movement of the 19th century was a social movement to end slavery and emancipate slaves. Slavery was an integral part of the American South. Most abolitionists were Northerners. They considered slavery a moral disease that threatened the Union. Abolitionists worked through political channels to free slaves and end the system of slavery. Some worked to help escaped slaves on the Underground Railroad. The turning point for the movement came in 1860 when Abraham Lincoln, who opposed the spread of slavery, became president of the United States.

AMERICAN PRISON REFORM

Zebulon Brockway and Dorothea Dix are two of the most prominent figures in the history of American prison reform. Brockway worked at or ran numerous prisons over his lifetime and was an advocate for prison education and training inmates with vocational skills. He also introduced the idea of parole. After spending many years visiting prisons, Dorothea could not bear the sights she had witnessed. It was not uncommon for men, women, and children to be grouped together in the same prison, and those that were sick were not provided with adequate medical care. She took particular note of the wretched state of those with mental illnesses, as they were chronically abused and mistreated. Through her efforts, mental asylums were established to better care for those with mental illnesses, and many states developed an independent system to better deal with children.

CARE FOR INDIVIDUALS WITH DISABILITIES

Much of the reform movements for the care of disabled individuals began towards the end of World War I. With so many injured and disabled veterans returning home from the war, the Fess-Smith Civilian Vocational Rehabilitation Act was passed in 1920 to try and meet the large spike in needs for the disabled. The Social Security Act, which was passed by President Franklin D. Roosevelt in 1935, included grants for state assistance programs for the blind and disabled children; however, this did not amend the discrimination still felt by disabled individuals as they were extremely less likely to be hired for employment. In response, the American Federation of the Physically Handicapped is formed in 1938 by Paul Strachan, as America's first cross-disability political organization. It lobbied extensively for fair employment for the disabled, including a National Employ the Physically Handicapped Week.

ATTITUDES TOWARD EDUCATION IN THE EARLY 19TH CENTURY

Horace Mann, among others, felt that schools could help children become better citizens, keep them away from crime, prevent poverty, and help American society become more unified. His *Common School Journal* brought his ideas of the importance of education into the public consciousness and proposed his suggestions for an improved American education system. Increased literacy led to increased awareness of current events, Western expansion, and other major developments of the time period. Public interest and participation in the arts and literature also increased. By the end of the 19th century, all children had access to a **free public elementary education**.

LABOR REFORM

Rapid industrialization in the late 19th century revolutionized how the workforce operated. The mass migration of workers to factories brought great economic gain, but it also brought hazardous

35

working conditions and unfair labor practices. The labor movement desired fair working hours and wages for the quickly growing labor force. Unions, such as the National Labor Union and the Knights of Labor, arose in the midst of these struggles to fight for the rights of workers across the nation. It was not until 1886, that Samuel Gompers founded the American Federation of Labor for skilled workers that ultimately established the union and labor movement as a force with real power to act as an agent of change. Safer working conditions began steadily increasing throughout different industries and work hours began decreasing towards the standard eight-hour workday we have today.

EARLY LEADERS IN THE WOMEN'S RIGHTS MOVEMENT

The women's rights movement began in the 1840s, with leaders including Elizabeth Cady Stanton, Sojourner Truth, Ernestine Rose, and Lucretia Mott. In 1869, Elizabeth Cady Stanton and Susan B. Anthony formed the **National Woman Suffrage Association**, fighting for women's right to vote.

In 1848, in Seneca Falls, the first women's rights convention was held, with about 300 attendees. The two-day **Seneca Falls Convention** discussed the rights of women to vote (suffrage) as well as equal treatment in careers, legal proceedings, etc. The convention produced a "Declaration of Sentiments," which outlined a plan for women to attain the rights they deserved. **Frederick Douglass** supported the women's rights movement, as well as the abolition movement. In fact, women's rights and abolition movements often went hand-in-hand during this time period.

> **Review Video: What was the Women's Rights Movement in America?**
> Visit mometrix.com/academy and enter code: 987734

TEMPERANCE MOVEMENT OF THE 19TH CENTURY

The temperance movement of the 19th century was a social movement, led mostly by women, to discourage the consumption of alcohol. As the movement gained ground in the mid-1800s, it changed from a purely social movement advocating moderation in the consumption of alcohol to a political movement that was successful in getting the government to regulate the sale of alcohol. The 18th Amendment to the Constitution established Prohibition, which made alcohol illegal in this country. Through this lens, the temperance movement of the 19th century was very successful in achieving its goals and had a significant impact on life in the United States. (The 18th Amendment was repealed by the 21st Amendment in 1933 and is the only constitutional amendment to have been repealed.)

W.E.B. DU BOIS'S WORK AS CIVIL RIGHTS ACTIVIST

Du Bois was the foremost intellectual and political activist for African-Americans in the 20th century's first half and was called "The Father of Pan-Africanism." He and educator Booker T. Washington collaborated on ideas for solutions to political disenfranchisement and segregation, and on organizing the "Negro Exhibition" showing black contributions to American society at Paris's 1900 Exposition Universelle. In 1905 he cofounded the Niagara Movement, championing free speech, voting, leadership, and antiracist ideals. Cofounder William Trotter felt whites should be excluded. Du Bois disagreed and cofounded the National Association for the Advancement of Colored People (NAACP) in 1909 where races could unite for civil rights. He left his faculty position at Atlanta University and became NAACP's publications director in 1910, publishing Harlem Renaissance writers Langston Hughes and Jean Toomer. Becoming more radical as NAACP became more institutionalized, Du Bois suggested black separatism as an economic policy in the 1930s and returned to teaching at Atlanta University. He corresponded with NAACP member Albert Einstein, who called racism "America's worst disease" in 1946.

THE GREAT AWAKENING

The Great Awakening was a religious revival in New England in the 1730s and 40s. It began in response to the growing secularism and was aided by the recent migrations into the cities, where it was easier for large crowds to form. Jonathan Edwards was one of the most famous preachers of this time. The Great Awakening was the first mass movement in America; it helped break down the divides between the various regions of the British colonies and led to the formation of some new Protestant denominations. Though the Revivalists did not directly advocate the abolition of slavery, they did suggest that there was divinity in all creation, and that therefore blacks were worthy of being converted to Christianity.

SECOND GREAT AWAKENING

Led by Protestant evangelical leaders, the Second Great Awakening occurred between 1800 and 1830. Several missionary groups grew out of the movement, including the American Home Missionary Society, which formed in 1826. The ideas behind the Second Great Awakening focused on personal responsibility, both as an individual and in response to injustice and suffering. The American Bible Society and the American Tract Society provided literature, while various traveling preachers spread the word. New religions arose, including the Latter-Day Saints and Seventh-Day Adventists.

THE TEMPERANCE MOVEMENT

Another movement associated with the Second Great Awakening was the temperance movement, focused on ending the production and use of alcohol. One major organization behind the temperance movement was the Society for the Promotion of Temperance, formed in 1826 in Boston, Massachusetts.

DEVELOPMENT OF AMERICAN ART

In the middle of the 19th century, several generations of landscape painters began depicting picturesque scenes of untouched American landscape. Hoping to capture the rugged and idyllic nature of America's raw wilderness, several of the artists built homes along the Hudson River to envelop themselves in the subject of much of their art. Although the term "Hudson River School" was initially meant to be derogatory by critics—because landscape painting was considered a lower form of artistic expression—the paintings captured the attention of Americans and quickly became the premiere style of American art into the 20th century. The painters had succeeded in not only producing awe-inspiring scenes, but also a style that was uniquely American.

Much of the American arts scene in the 19th century reflected unchanging American ideals and beliefs—that America was a blessed land filled with endless resources. It reinforced the continuity of the everyday worker's agricultural life and the unchanging majesty of its geography. And yet, it also reflected the changes and progress America was making as it expanded West—constantly pursuing its manifest destiny and gaining dominion over previously untamed frontier land. Writers, poets, painters, and musicians all began to develop styles that were wholly their own, and yet still distinctly American in their themes and content.

THE BATTLE HYMN OF THE REPUBLIC

The Battle Hymn of the Republic was written by Julia Ward Howe. The hymn used the music from the song *John Brown's Body*, but Howe's more famous lyrics quickly became the words most commonly associated with the tune. The song, which makes reference to the Biblical final judgment of the wicked, was sung as a campfire song by Union soldiers during the Civil War, and became a prominent American patriotic song.

TRANSCENDENTALISM

Transcendentalism was a religious and philosophical movement that came about during the first half of the 19th century. It began as a general protest against the state of the culture and society, and in particular against the intellectualism popular at the time. At the most basic levels, the Transcendentalists believed that people were inherently good, as was nature in general. They also believed that certain institutions, primarily organized religion and politics, corrupted the purity of the individual and, as such, should be avoided. Transcendentalism held to the view that religion was not subject to empirical proof, and could be based simply on one's own personal individual experience.

Government and Citizenship

GOVERNMENT
MAGNA CARTA AND THE ENGLISH BILL OF RIGHTS

The Magna Carta was an English charter that was put into law in 1215 and then revised in 1297. It was the first document to limit the powers of the English king (King John) and grant liberties to certain citizens. It also mandated that free persons could only be punished according to the law of the land. The Magna Carta contributed to the development of constitutional law and inspired the creation of the United States Constitution.

The English Bill of Rights was passed by English Parliament in 1689. It prevented the king from suspending laws and forced royalty to abide by the laws of parliament. It influenced the United States Bill of Rights, specifically the right to trial by jury and the prohibition of excessive bail and cruel and unusual punishment.

ARTICLES OF CONFEDERATION

The Articles of Confederation were the first Constitution of the United States. When fully ratified in 1781, it established a union of the states. Some of the strengths of the Articles of Confederation are that it created a union in which states could act together to declare war and negotiate agreements. The major weakness of the document was that the federal government could not collect taxes. Each state had to agree to give the federal government funds. In addition, the document did not create a fair balance between the large and small states in terms of legislative decision-making and funding. Each state was given one vote, but large states were expected to contribute more money.

> **Review Video: What were the Articles of Confederation?**
> Visit mometrix.com/academy and enter code: 927401

DECLARATION OF INDEPENDENCE

The 13 colonies asserted their independence from England in 1776 with the adoption of the Declaration of Independence. In June 1776, Congress appointed a committee to draft a document to explain to the world why the colonies wanted independence. The goal was to gain international support. The document that was created was the Declaration of Independence, which argued for the "unalienable rights" of all people, among other things. On July 4, 1776, the Declaration of Independence was approved by all of the representatives from all 13 colonies.

> **Review Video: What is the Declaration of Independence?**
> Visit mometrix.com/academy and enter code: 256838

SEPARATION OF POWERS

Separation of powers means that the government has three branches: legislative, executive, and judicial. Through a system of checks and balances, these branches work together and none is allowed to become too powerful. The separation of powers is granted in the U.S. Constitution. The Constitution states that Congress has the "legislative powers herein granted" and lists the actions in Article I, Section 8, that Congress is allowed to take. The next section lists those actions that are prohibited for Congress to take. Article II describes the powers of the executive branch, including the president, and Article III gives judicial power to the Supreme Court.

REPUBLICANISM AND INDIVIDUAL RIGHTS

Republicanism is a governing philosophy that emphasizes individual liberty, inalienable rights, and popular sovereignty. It rejects inherited power and government corruption. Republicanism and democracy are not the same. In a democracy, the majority can vote to remove rights from a minority group. However, in a republic, every person is granted certain inalienable rights that cannot be taken away by anyone. The Constitution protected the rights of individuals by incorporating certain republican elements. The Constitution:

- Created a senate that was controlled by the states.
- Established an electoral college to elect the president rather than relying on a straight popular vote.
- Preserved the sovereignty of individual states.
- Required a super majority to amend the Constitution.

Individual rights are held by the citizens of a country, and cannot be taken away by any person or group without due process. The Constitution enumerates the individual rights of U.S. citizens within the Bill of Rights.

IMPACT OF THOMAS HOOKER

Thomas Hooker was a Puritan preacher and theologian who is known as the "Father of Connecticut." After disagreements arose between himself and another famous pastor John Cotton, he and a group of settlers moved to the soon to be formed Connecticut colony in a town they would call Hartford. It soon became time to establish a rule of law, and in 1638, a general court prepared for a written form of law at roughly the same time the First Church of Hartford opened. Hooker preached the opening sermon establishing that the foundation of any authority can only be maintained at the consent of **free people**. It is believed that this sermon drastically influenced the town's constitution that was to be written, named the "Fundamental Orders of Connecticut." Historian John Fiske once asserted that this was "the first written constitution known to history that created a government. It marked the beginnings of American democracy, of which Thomas Hooker deserves more than any other man to be called the father. The government of the United States today is in lineal descent more nearly related to that of Connecticut than to that of any of the other thirteen colonies."

CONTRIBUTIONS OF JOHN LOCKE, MONTESQUIEU, AND ROUSSEAU TO POLITICAL SCIENCE

John Locke published *Two Treatises of Government* in 1689. This work argued against the ideas of Thomas Hobbes. He put forth the theory of *tabula rasa*—that people are born with minds like blank slates. Individual minds are molded by experience, not innate knowledge or intuition. He also believed that all men should be independent and equal. Many of Locke's ideas found their way into the Constitution of the United States.

The two French philosophers, **Montesquieu** and **Rousseau**, heavily influenced the French Revolution (1789-1799). They believed government policies and ideas should change to alleviate existing problems, an idea referred to as "liberalism." Rousseau, in particular, directly influenced the Revolution with writings such as *The Social Contract* (1762) and *Declaration of the Rights of Man and of the Citizen* (1789). Other ideas Rousseau and Montesquieu espoused included:

- Individual freedom and community welfare are of equal importance
- Man's innate goodness leads to natural harmony
- Reason develops with the rise of civilized society
- Individual citizens carry certain obligations to the existing government

CHANGING THE U.S. CONSTITUTION

The U.S. Constitution can be changed but only through the difficult process of amendment. The first step is for a bill to pass both houses of Congress--the Senate and the House of Representatives--by a two-thirds majority in each. This is no easy task. Next, the bill must go to the states for approval. The amendment must be approved by three-fourths of the states. Usually, this is done in the state legislatures by a simple majority vote. If three-fourths of the states approve the amendment, it becomes part of the U.S. Constitution. The president of the United States has no formal role in the amendment process. Only 27 amendments have been added in the history of the U.S. Constitution.

13TH, 14TH, AND 15TH AMENDMENTS

The 13th, 14th and 15th amendments were passed during the Reconstruction era after the Civil War ended. The 13th amendment to the U.S. Constitution freed all slaves and legally forbade slavery in the United States. Slaves were freed without giving monetary compensation to the slaveholders. The fact that slavery was made illegal has had a huge impact on life in the United States, altering the societal composition of Southern states as well as some border states.

14TH AMENDMENT

The 14th amendment declared that all persons born or naturalized (except Native American Indians) were U.S. citizens and that all citizens were entitled to equal rights regardless of race. Most of the Confederate states were forced to comply based on the Military Reconstruction Act. The amendment fell short of giving black men the right to vote but paved the way for the 15th amendment. It angered women's rights activists because it made the right to vote a male right. The major impact of the 14th amendment was that human rights were granted at the state as well as the national level through the "due process clause."

15TH AMENDMENT

The 15th amendment granted black men the right to vote. Like the 14th amendment, it passed because Confederate states were forced to comply based on the Military Reconstruction Act. Women's rights activists opposed the amendment because it granted the right to vote to males only. Women weren't granted the right to vote until the passage of the 19th amendment. The 13th, 14th and 15th amendments had a huge impact on life in the United States because they put an end to the era of slavery and were the first steps in giving freedom and equal rights to black people at the state and national levels.

OBJECTIONS AGAINST THE CONSTITUTION

Once the Constitution was drafted, it was presented for approval by the states. Nine states needed to approve the document for it to become official. However, debate and discussion continued. Major **concerns** included:

- There was no bill of rights to protect individual freedoms.
- States felt too much power was being handed over to the central government.
- Voters wanted more control over their elected representatives.

Discussion about necessary changes to the Constitution was divided into two camps: Federalists and Anti-Federalists. **Federalists** wanted a strong central government. **Anti-Federalists** wanted to prevent a tyrannical government from developing if a central government held too much power.

MAJOR PLAYERS IN THE FEDERALIST AND ANTI-FEDERALIST CAMPS

Major Federalist leaders included Alexander Hamilton, John Jay, and James Madison. They wrote a series of letters, called the **Federalist Papers**, aimed at convincing the states to ratify the Constitution. These were published in New York papers. Anti-Federalists included Thomas Jefferson and Patrick Henry. They argued against the Constitution as it was originally drafted in a series of **Anti-Federalist Papers**.

The final compromise produced a strong central government controlled by checks and balances. A **Bill of Rights** was also added, becoming the first ten amendments to the Constitution. These amendments protected rights such as freedom of speech, freedom of religion, and other basic rights. Aside from various amendments added throughout the years, the United States Constitution has remained unchanged.

CONTRIBUTIONS OF GEORGE MASON

George Mason is perhaps the most overlooked of the early contributors to American politics. Both James Madison and Thomas Jefferson frequently deferred to him when it came to questions on civics, and he was a close friend of George Washington for most of his life. He also wrote the Virginia Declaration of Rights, which was one of the most influential documents of the time, with its ideals infused into many state constitutions, as well as into the Declaration of Independence that would be written only a few weeks later. Mason's understanding and declaration of the inherent rights of man are so synonymously tied to the ideals of America, that it is difficult to understate just how influential he was in the formation of the United States. However, his most famous action was his refusal to sign the original Constitution presented at the Constitutional Congress in 1787, because, "There [was] no Declaration of Rights." This became a common chant for Anti-Federalists who agreed with Mason's reluctance to sign a document when he believed that "it is at present impossible to foresee whether it will, in its operation, produce a monarchy or a corrupt oppressive aristocracy: it will most probably vibrate some years between the two, and then terminate in the one or the other."

JACKSONIAN DEMOCRACY VS. PRECEDING POLITICAL CLIMATE

Jacksonian Democracy is largely seen as a shift from politics favoring the wealthy to politics favoring the common man. The right to **vote** was give to all free white males, not just property owners, as had been the case previously. Jackson's approach favored the patronage system, laissez-faire economics, and relocation of the Indian tribes from the Southeast portion of the country. Jackson opposed the formation of a federal bank and allowed the Second Bank of the United States to collapse by vetoing a bill to renew the charter. Jackson also faced the challenge of the **Nullification Crisis** when South Carolina claimed that it could ignore or nullify any federal law it considered unconstitutional. Jackson sent troops to the state to enforce the protested tariff laws, and a compromise engineered by Henry Clay in 1833 settled the matter for the time being.

LANDMARK SUPREME COURT CASES

The Supreme Court led by John Marshall is credited with increasing the power of the national government over that of the states. This court also gave the judicial branch more power and prestige, notably in the case of Marbury v. Madison (1803). Marshall was known as an arch-Federalist, and as a loose interpreter of the Constitution. In the case McCullough v. Maryland (1819), the court ruled that a national bank is allowed by the Constitution, and that states cannot tax a federal agency. In the case of Gibbons v. Ogden (1824), the right of Congress to regulate interstate commerce was reaffirmed, and indeed federal regulation of just about anything was made possible. In Fletcher v. Peck (1810), the sanctity of contracts was asserted; this case also established the right of the Supreme Court to declare state laws unconstitutional.

> **Review Video: Marbury v. Madison**
> Visit mometrix.com/academy and enter code: 573964

MARBURY V. MADISON

Marbury v. Madison was the first Supreme Court judgment that supported the federal system of government. In 1803 this landmark case established the principle of judicial review, which means the judiciary can determine that a law is unconstitutional. The principle of judicial review gives more power to the U.S. Constitution than to the legislature, because laws created and passed by the legislature may still be deemed unconstitutional. William Marbury was denied his claim regarding his appointment as a justice of the peace because the U.S. Supreme Court determined that the statute on which he based his claim was unconstitutional. This case helped define the system of checks and balances.

DRED SCOTT DECISION

Abolitionist factions coalesced around the case of **Dred Scott**, using his case to test the country's laws regarding slavery. Scott, a slave, had been taken by his owner from Missouri, which was a slave state. He then traveled to Illinois, a free state, then on to the Minnesota Territory, also free based on the Missouri Compromise. After several years, he returned to Missouri, and his owner subsequently died. Abolitionists took Scott's case to court, stating that Scott was no longer a slave but free, since he had lived in free territory. The case went to the Supreme Court.

The Supreme Court stated that, because Scott, as a slave, was not a US citizen, his time in free states did not change his status. He also did not have the right to sue. In addition, the Court determined that the **Missouri Compromise** was unconstitutional, stating that Congress had overstepped its bounds by outlawing slavery in the territories.

> **Review Video: What was the Dred Scott Decision?**
> Visit mometrix.com/academy and enter code: 364838

CITIZENSHIP

UNALIENABLE RIGHTS

The term unalienable rights refers to the fundamental rights that are guaranteed to people naturally instead of by law. People have certain natural rights, and laws cannot take them away. The Declaration of Independence stated that these unalienable rights are: "life, liberty, and the pursuit of happiness." The Bill of Rights, which is the first 10 amendments to the Constitution, lists religious freedom, freedom of speech and of the press, and the right to assemble and petition as additional unalienable rights that people possess.

RIGHTS GUARANTEED BY THE BILL OF RIGHTS

The Bill of Rights is composed of the first ten amendments to the U.S. Constitution. The ten amendments were passed on December 15, 1791. The rights that are protected by each amendment are listed here:

- Freedom of religion, speech, press, peaceable assembly, and government petition.
- The right to bear arms.
- Protection from the quartering of soldiers in private homes except by law during wartime.
- Protection from unreasonable search and seizure.
- Due process and protection from double jeopardy and self-incrimination.
- The right of the accused to a speedy, public criminal trial before an impartial jury.
- The right to a civil trial by jury in accord with common law.
- Protection from cruel and unusual punishment and excessive fines and bail.
- The preservation of rights not mentioned.
- The preservation of the rights of states and individuals.

US CITIZENSHIP
QUALIFICATIONS OF A US CITIZEN/HOW CITIZENSHIP MAY BE LOST

Anyone born in the US, born abroad to a US citizen, or who has gone through a process of naturalization is considered a **citizen** of the United States. It is possible to lose US citizenship as a result of conviction of certain crimes such as treason. Citizenship may also be lost if a citizen pledges an oath to another country or serves in the military of a country engaged in hostilities with the US. A US citizen can also choose to hold dual citizenship, work as an expatriate in another country without losing US citizenship, or even to renounce citizenship if he or she so chooses.

RIGHTS, DUTIES, AND RESPONSIBILITIES GRANTED TO OR EXPECTED FROM CITIZENS

Citizens are granted certain rights under the US government. The most important of these are defined in the **Bill of Rights**, and include freedom of speech, religion, assembly, and a variety of other rights the government is not allowed to remove. A US citizen also has a number of **duties**:

- Paying taxes
- Loyalty to the government (though the US does not prosecute those who criticize or seek to change the government)
- Support and defense of the Constitution
- Serving in the Armed Forces when required by law
- Obeying laws as set forth by the various levels of government.

Responsibilities of a US citizen include:

- Voting in elections
- Respecting one another's rights and not infringing on them
- Staying informed about various political and national issues
- Respecting one another's beliefs

FOUNDING FATHERS AS MODELS OF CIVIC VIRTUE

The Founding Fathers did not declare their independence lightly. These were all well-intentioned men truly seeking the best type of society of which they believed human kind was capable. To them,

civic virtue was a necessary intellectual foundation to establish their ideal republic. The only way they determined that society could flourish was if every citizen was devoted to the success of the greater community above their own personal interests. John Adams said, "We ought to consider what is the end [purpose] of government before we determine which is the best form. Upon this point all speculative politicians will agree that the happiness of society is the end of government, as all divines and moral philosophers will agree that the happiness of the individual is the end of man. …All sober inquirers after truth, ancient and modern, pagan and Christian, have declared that the happiness of man, as well as his dignity, consists in virtue."

CIVIL DISOBEDIENCE IN US HISTORY

It is precisely because of the Founding Father's civic virtue that deciding to declare themselves an independent and sovereign nation took so much debate. They had determined that in order to be virtuous, they must be willing to stand out against what they believed was unjust. The Boston Tea Party is a commonly referenced example of people being civilly disobedient—choosing to do that which is considered unlawful, in order to do what they believe is right. Henry David Thoreau was famously arrested for refusing to pay for a poll tax that he believed would support the institution of slavery, of which he was radically opposed. Though the fine for his "crime" was paid without his knowing, Thoreau was so upset about the situation that he would go on to write an essay entitled *Civil Disobedience* to explain his actions and what he believed should be the actions of all men who claim to be just. This writing would be the intellectual foundation of both Mohandas K. Gandhi and Martin Luther King Jr.'s movements years later.

EFFECT OF POLITICAL PARTIES ON THE FUNCTIONING OF AN INDIVIDUAL GOVERNMENT

Different types and numbers of political parties can have a significant effect on how a government is run. If there is a **single party**, or a one-party system, the government is defined by that one party, and all policy is based on that party's beliefs. In a **two-party system**, two parties with different viewpoints compete for power and influence. The US is basically a two-party system, with checks and balances to make it difficult for one party to gain complete power over the other. There are also **multiparty systems**, with three or more parties. In multiparty systems, various parties will often come to agreements in order to form a majority and shift the balance of power.

DEVELOPMENT OF POLITICAL PARTIES IN THE US.

George Washington was adamantly against the establishment of **political parties**, based on the abuses perpetrated by such parties in Britain. However, political parties developed in US politics almost from the beginning. Major parties throughout US history have included:

- **Federalists and Democratic-Republicans**—these parties formed in the late 1700s and disagreed on the balance of power between national and state government.
- **Democrats and Whigs**—these developed in the 1830s, and many political topics of the time centered on national economic issues.
- **Democrats and Republicans**—the Republican Party developed before the Civil War, after the collapse of the Whig party, and the two parties debated issues centering on slavery and economic issues, such as taxation.

While third parties sometimes enter the picture in US politics, the government is basically a two-party system, dominated by the Democrats and Republicans.

FUNCTIONS OF POLITICAL PARTIES

Political parties form organizations at all levels of government. Activities of individual parties include:

- Recruiting and backing candidates for offices
- Discussing various issues with the public, increasing public awareness
- Working toward compromise on difficult issues
- Staffing government offices and providing administrative support

At the administrative level, parties work to ensure that viable candidates are available for elections and that offices and staff are in place to support candidates as they run for office and afterward, when they are elected.

FREE SPEECH

Freedom of speech is one of the rights protected by the Bill of Rights, which is the first 10 amendments to the U.S. Constitution. Freedom of speech is crucial to a democratic society because each person is allowed to say whatever he or she thinks, even something negative about the government of the country. This freedom allows critics of governmental policies to voice their concerns without fear of reprisals. Having open discourse about the policies and laws of the country is one of the hallmarks of a free and democratic society.

IMPORTANCE OF FREE PRESS AND THE MEDIA

The right to free speech guaranteed in the first amendment to the Constitution allows the media to report on **government and political activities** without fear of retribution. Because the media has access to information about the government, the government's policies and actions, and debates and discussions that occur in Congress, it can keep the public informed about the inner workings of the government. The media can also draw attention to injustices, imbalances of power, and other transgressions the government or government officials might commit. However, media outlets may, like special interest groups, align themselves with certain political viewpoints and skew their reports to fit that viewpoint. The rise of the **internet** has made media reporting even more complex, as news can be found from an infinite variety of sources, both reliable and unreliable.

EFFECTS OF THE MISSOURI COMPROMISE ON THE TENSIONS BETWEEN THE NORTH AND SOUTH

By 1819, the United States had developed a tenuous balance between slave and free states, with exactly 22 senators in Congress from each faction. However, Missouri was ready to join the union. As a slave state, it would tip the balance in Congress. To prevent this imbalance, the **Missouri Compromise** brought the northern part of Massachusetts into the union as Maine, establishing it as a free state to balance the admission of Missouri as a slave state. In addition, the remaining portion of the Louisiana Purchase was to remain free north of **latitude 36°30'**. Since cotton did not grow well this far north, this limitation was acceptable to congressmen representing the slave states.

However, the proposed Missouri constitution presented a problem, as it outlawed immigration of free blacks into the state. Another compromise was in order, this time proposed by **Henry Clay**. According to this new compromise, Missouri would never pass a law that prevented anyone from entering the state. Through this and other work, Clay earned his title of the "**Great Compromiser**."

> **Review Video: What was the Missouri Compromise?**
> Visit mometrix.com/academy and enter code: 848091

POPULAR SOVEREIGNTY AND THE COMPROMISE OF 1850

In addition to the pro-slavery and anti-slavery factions, a third group rose, who felt that each individual state should decide whether to allow or permit slavery within its borders. The idea that a state could make its own choices was referred to as **popular sovereignty**.

When California applied to join the union in 1849, the balance of congressional power was again threatened. The **Compromise of 1850** introduced a group of laws meant to bring an end to the conflict:

- California's admittance as a free state
- The outlaw of the slave trade in Washington, DC
- An increase in efforts to capture escaped slaves
- The right of New Mexico and Utah territories to decide individually whether to allow slavery

In spite of these measures, debate raged each time a new state prepared to enter the union.

KANSAS-NEBRASKA ACT TRIGGER OF ADDITIONAL CONFLICT

With the creation of the Kansas and Nebraska territories in 1854, another debate began. Congress allowed popular sovereignty in these territories, but slavery opponents argued that the Missouri Compromise had already made slavery illegal in this region. In Kansas, two separate governments arose, one pro-slavery and one anti-slavery. Conflict between the two factions rose to violence, leading Kansas to gain the nickname of "**Bleeding Kansas**."

> **Review Video: Sectional Crisis: The Kansas-Nebraska Act**
> Visit mometrix.com/academy and enter code: 982119

ADMIRABLE QUALITIES IN AMERICAN HISTORY
GEORGE WASHINGTON

George Washington is often referred to as one of the greatest leaders in our nation's history. Despite numerous losses in battle in both the French and Indian and Revolutionary Wars, he maintained a reputation as a commander worthy of honor. Though Washington was not formally educated, John Adams vouched for his character as the man who should lead the Continental Army. Most of his peers agreed that he had a tall and commanding figure that was both graceful and calm, and it was common for Washington to end up mediating or leading an event without ever asking to. He was self-disciplined and insisted on not being paid for his work. It is interesting to note, however, that John Adams did not particularly like Washington by the time he was elected president, and not even after his death. Adams believed much of Washington's praise came simply because he was tall, handsome, inherited wealth, and was Virginian by birth. Regardless, Washington held the respect of every Founding Father, and it is unlikely that America would have succeeded without his leadership.

JOHN MARSHALL

John Marshall, a second cousin of Thomas Jefferson, is most well-known for his role as a justice for the Supreme Court. During his appointment, he helped establish the judicial branch of government as a viable and equal entity that was able to provide checks and balances to the other branches of the federal government. In the landmark case, <u>Marbury v. Madison</u>, the idea of judicial review was instated and essentially made the Supreme Court the final authority in determining whether something was constitutional. He is widely considered one of the most influential Supreme Court justices in American history.

QUALITIES OF ABRAHAM LINCOLN

Abraham Lincoln was the 16th, and perhaps greatest, President of the United States. He is typically described as one of America's greatest leaders for his efforts during the most divisive time in United States history. Much like George Washington, he was a tall man that radiated a peace and calm. It was said that he often wrote letters he never planned to send to those he disagreed with rather than be harsh with them in person. He was known to fill his cabinet with those who disagreed with him, even his presidential opponent, William Seward, who became one of his most trusted advisors. Though he had very little formal education, he established himself as a successful lawyer and always seemed to be able to clearly communicate his goals and aspirations for those he served. His steadfast conviction and gentle mannerisms kept the Union from breaking apart as it fought with the Confederacy to reestablish what Lincoln believed in all along—a fully United States.

SUSAN B. ANTHONY

In her twenties, Anthony was a schoolteacher and then a headmistress. Observing that men teachers' wages were four times those of women inspired her to fight for equal pay. Before the Civil War, she worked for temperance and antislavery movements. Reading of the first National Women's Rights Convention in 1850 and Horace Greeley's admiration of a speech by Lucy Stone, Anthony was inspired by Stone's speech to dedicate her life to women's rights, later meeting Greeley and Stone in 1852. In 1851, after a convention's denying her admission for being female, Anthony organized America's first women's state temperance society with Elizabeth Cady Stanton. Thereafter they crossed the country speaking together for women's equal treatment. They founded the National Woman Suffrage Association (NWSA) in 1869. Anthony's 1872 arrest, trial, and conviction for voting illegally gave her an even bigger audience for women's suffrage. Anthony co-published The History of Women's Suffrage (1884–1887). In 1890, she engineered NWSA's merger with Stone's AWSA, forming the NAWSA.

ELIZABETH CADY STANTON

Elizabeth Cady Stanton was the author of the Declaration of Rights of Women. She spent her life working for the rights of women, especially the right to vote. Working with Lucretia Mott, she organized the Seneca Falls Women's Rights Convention, where she wrote the Declaration of Rights. She pushed the assembly to adopt a resolution calling for women to gain the right to vote. Stanton was an important thinker in the women's rights movement, in addition to being a wife and mother of seven children.

FREDERICK DOUGLASS

Frederick Douglass endured difficulties from the beginning of his early childhood. At a young age, Douglass witnessed his aunt beaten until she was bloodied, and he recalls being cold and hungry much of the time. At age 7 or 8, he was sent to live with Mr. and Mrs. Hugh Auld in Baltimore. Mrs. Auld attempted to teach him how to read but was rebuked by her husband. He watched slavery turn her from a kind person into a bitter slaveholder. His darkest time, however, was when he was sent to live with Edward Covey, where he was constantly beaten and overworked. Later at a shipyard, he was beaten by some of the white workers, but eventually learned to calk, and settled in New Bedford, Massachusetts as a free man. He became one of the most influential speakers against slavery in American history and a leader in the abolitionist movement. While perhaps most well-known for his autobiography and his fiery oratory, his work in journalism also played a significant role in the anti-slavery movement. His primary contribution to journalism was as publisher of the North Star, a newspaper published from 1847 to 1851. Frederick Douglass supported the women's rights movement, as well as the abolition movement. In fact, women's rights and abolition movements often went hand-in-hand through this time period.

JOHN PAUL JONES

John Paul Jones was a pirate to the English but a hero to America. Jones was a Scottish-American who rose to prominence through numerous skirmishes and victories at sea during the Revolutionary War. A bit of a checkered past, Jones came to America after fleeing trial for defending himself from a mutinous crew that he ultimately killed in self-defense. Jones was given command of various different vessels during his command, but his most famous was the flagship *Bonhomme Richard*. Jones frequently led squadrons into the English countryside and against their merchant ships, which led to him being recognized as a "Blackbeard-like" pirate to the British populace. In 1779, Jones engaged the Royal Navy frigate *Serapis* in one of the bloodiest naval battles in history. Although the *Bonhomme Richard* had begun to sink and was ablaze, Jones refused to surrender, saying, "I have not yet begun to fight." His endurance prevailed, and eventually the *Serapis* surrendered; Jones then took command of the *Serapis* as his ship sank into the sea. He became known as the "Father of the American Navy."

BECOMING A NATURALIZED CITIZEN OF THE UNITED STATES

Naturalization is the acquisition of citizenship of a country by a person who was not previously a citizen of that country. There are several ways to qualify for citizenship through naturalization in the United States. A legal resident alien may apply for US citizenship after living as a permanent resident of the US for at least 5 years, or 3 years while married to a US citizen. Alternatively, serving a designated period of time in the US Armed Forces qualifies one to apply for citizenship after only 1 year of permanent residency. Once one of these qualifications is met, a person may apply and will be required to pass a citizenship test.

WOMEN'S RIGHTS MOVEMENT

The women's rights movement began in the 1840s with leaders including Elizabeth Cady Stanton, Ernestine Rose and Lucretia Mott. Later, in 1869, the National Woman Suffrage Association, fighting for women's right to vote, came into being. It was led by Susan B. Anthony, Ernestine Rose and Elizabeth Cady Stanton. In 1848 in Seneca Falls, the first women's rights convention was held, with about three hundred attendees. The Seneca Falls Convention brought to the floor the issue that women could not vote or run for office. The convention produced a "Declaration of Sentiments" which outlined a plan for women to attain the rights they deserved. Frederick Douglass supported the women's rights movement, as well as the abolition movement. In fact, women's rights and abolition movements often went hand-in-hand through this time period.

DIFFERENT VIEWS OF TARIFF POLICIES

The issue of trade and tariffs created significant differences between the North and South that led to the Civil War. The North had a domestic economy and viewed foreign trade as competition. When foreign goods are taxed at a higher rate, the goods become more expensive and less competitive. For this reason, Northerners argued in favor of protective tariffs. The South, on the other hand, was very dependent on imported manufactured goods from Europe. The South also exported much of its agricultural goods. For these reasons, the South was opposed to protective tariffs, which made goods more expensive for Southerners to buy. The disagreement over protective tariffs led to the Nullification Crisis of 1832 when South Carolina declared the tariffs null and void within its state borders.

Economics, Science, Technology, and Society

ECONOMICS
ECONOMY IN THE SOUTH

Because of its long growing season, the South's economy utilized cash crops intended for export. The most important crops grown in the Southern colonies during the colonial period were rice and tobacco, along with indigo, and sugar before most of the South began switching to cotton in the early 1800s. Most of the food for the nation was grown in the mid-Atlantic colonies, and the North East manufactured textiles because it lacked proper soil to maintain steady yields of crops. More fertile than New England, the Middle Colonies became major producers of crops including rye, oats, potatoes, wheat, and barley. Some particularly wealthy inhabitants owned large farms and/or businesses and were able to produce enough to have a surplus to sell.

SOUTHERN CLIMATE

The American South had a warm climate and a long growing season. It was ideal for many different cash crops, like indigo and rice. Tobacco was a difficult crop that rapidly removed nutrients from the soil. But if done well, it could generate large sums of money. However, with the invention of the cotton gin, and the growth of textile mills in Britain and the Northeastern U.S., cotton became an extremely lucrative crop. Because cotton was easy to grow and didn't deplete the soil, most farmers in the South readily switch to growing cotton instead of tobacco. The South relied on agriculture much more than did the Northern states. Growing and harvesting crops requires much manpower. For this reason, Southern whites depended on slaves. This economic dependence allowed slavery to become an integral part of Southern life, which, in turn, led to sharp differences between the North and South, and, eventually, the Civil War.

PLANTATION SYSTEM

The plantation system was the main method of agricultural production in the South. Plantations were large farms that had 20 or more slaves and produced one staple crop (i.e., rice, cotton, tobacco, or sugar). Much financial gain could be made by growing and selling these crops. However, such crops were very labor-intensive to grow and harvest. Plantation owners made the system

49

Copyright © Mometrix Media. You have been licensed one copy of this document for personal use only. Any other reproduction or redistribution is strictly prohibited. All rights reserved. This content is provided for test preparation purposes only and does not imply an endorsement by Mometrix of any particular political, scientific, or religious point of view.

profitable by having slaves who were basically free labor. Plantation owners thus owned the land, the tools, and the labor force. This allowed them to make more money.

TRANSATLANTIC SLAVE TRADE

The transatlantic slave trade was the industry of buying and selling slaves carried over from the African continent during the 16th through 19th centuries. The slaves were mostly West Africans kidnapped by rival African tribes and sold to European traders who transported them by ship to the New World. Slaves were a valuable commodity because, once purchased, a slave represented free labor for life. The American colonies, and later the United States, received a relatively small percentage of the slaves transported to the new world (only about 6%), the majority of whom were sold in the agricultural South. Southerners eventually came to depend on slaves to maintain their farms and plantations, ensuring continued demand for the slave trade.

ECONOMIC REASONS FOR RAPID INDUSTRIALIZATION

Rapid industrialization in the United States occurred during the Industrial Revolution of the 19th century (1820-1870). The Embargo Act of 1807 stopped the export of American goods and made the import of goods very difficult. Trade essentially came to a halt. This meant that the United States needed to become more independent, and the way to do so was to become more industrial. Manufacturing began to expand, and the government protected American manufacturing by passing a protective tariff on foreign-made goods. As factories and industries grew, domestic goods could be produced more quickly and cheaply.

FREE ENTERPRISE SYSTEM

The term "free enterprise system" refers to the capitalist system of economics. In a capitalist society, businesses are privately owned and goods are traded in markets. In a purely free enterprise, or market, system, everything can be owned privately. The government does not own anything or interfere in the private sector in any way. In a free market system, the individual can make his or her own economic choices without government involvement. People can choose what to produce, how to produce, how many to produce, and for whom to produce. Business owners can decide how to structure their businesses. Competition between companies is central to the free enterprise system.

SCIENCE, TECHNOLOGY, AND SOCIETY
TECHNOLOGICAL INNOVATIONS IN THE 19TH CENTURY

Technological innovations in the 19th century were instrumental in changing the way goods were manufactured. The most important innovation may well have been the cotton gin. Eli Whitney's invention made it possible to separate cotton seeds from the fiber of the plant. Previous to his invention, this task had been very time-consuming and labor- intensive. Because of the cotton gin, the South was able to send more cotton fiber to the North to be made into cloth. New processes for manufacturing cloth and the invention of the sewing machine enabled the textile industry to flourish in the North. The cotton gin is an example of the new way in which machines were used to manufacture goods at a much faster rate than humans could do on their own.

MORSE TELEGRAPH

The Morse telegraph was patented by Samuel F. B. Morse in the United States in 1837. The telegraph was a gigantic leap forward in the realm of communications. Before the telegraph, messages could take days, weeks or months to reach their intended recipient, based upon the distance that they had to travel. The telegraph allowed people to send messages through use of electric signals transmitted over telegraph wires, allowing for instantaneous communications. The main drawbacks to the telegraph included the need to "translate" the message into and out of the appropriate telegraphic code and that the telegraph could only relay one message at a time. By 1861, the Morse/Vail telegraph (Alfred Vail was Morse's assistant) had replaced the Pony Express as it reached from the East Coast of the country to the West Coast. The field-telegraph system was first used in the Civil War, and the Civil War was also the first war to see the use of the electrical telegraph. The field-telegraph system proved to be a major advantage to the Union because the Union had a stronger telegraph system than the Confederates.

COTTON GIN

Eli Whitney is best remembered for his invention of the Cotton Engine (shortened to "Gin") and his advocacy for interchangeable parts. Whitney received an order for 10,000 muskets for the U.S. government to be produced in two years. Up to that point, muskets had been handmade individually, making their production very slow. However, Whitney was able to fill the order by standardizing each part and then mass producing 10,000 copies of every part, advancing the development of mass production greatly. Whitney realized that it was more efficient to replace individual broken parts instead of the more costly replacement of an entire item if one section broke. He first applied interchangeable parts to musket production, but the concept soon spread to all types of manufacturing industries. This type of widespread mass production began to shift the United States into the era of rapid industrialization known as the Industrial Revolution.

IMPACT OF THE MISSISSIPPI RIVER

The Mississippi River was acquired by the United States in the Louisiana Purchase and is the largest river in North America. People live near rivers because they provide water for agriculture and a means to transport goods for economic gain. When the United States gained control over the Mississippi, many people moved westward and settled on its banks. During the 19th century, steamboats traveled up and down the river, bringing goods to the people who lived along its banks and taking exports to sell in other places. New Orleans developed as a major port city, and other cities, such as St. Louis, grew and thrived because of their location on the banks of the Mississippi River.

TRANSPORTATION SYSTEMS AND URBANIZATION

The Industrial Revolution had brought many industries and factories to cities. The growth of the transportation systems, mainly railroad and steamships, led to urbanization by increasing trade and making it possible to bring raw materials from the West to the factories in the East. This enabled the industries and factories to be successful and to grow. People wanted to be a part of these growing industries. Countless Americans moved from their farms to the cities because that is where the economic opportunities were.

HOMESTEAD ACT

The US government tried many different ways to improve conditions for farmers in the West. Under the Homestead Act of 1862, farmers were sold 160 acres for $10, with the proviso that they had to improve the land within 5 years. Between the years 1865 and 1900, only one in six farms began this way. The Timber Culture Act of 1873 gave more land to farmers, with the proviso that they had to plant some trees on that land.

One thing that helped to populate the West was the completion of the Transcontinental Railroad in 1869. The Union Pacific met the Central Pacific railway at Promontory Point, Utah. In 1889, the US government opened Oklahoma for settlement, and by 1893 it was completely settled.

DEVELOPMENTS IN TRANSPORTATION

As America expanded its borders, it also developed new technology to travel the rapidly growing country. Roads and railroads traversed the nation, with the **Transcontinental Railroad** eventually allowing travel from one coast to the other. Canals and steamboats simplified water travel and made shipping easier and less expensive. The **Erie Canal** (1825) connected the Great Lakes to the Hudson River. Other canals connected other major waterways, further facilitating transportation and the shipment of goods.

With growing numbers of settlers moving into the West, **wagon trails** developed, including the Oregon Trail, California Trail, and the Santa Fe Trail. The most common vehicles seen along these westbound trails were covered wagons, also known as **prairie schooners**.

INDUSTRIAL ACTIVITY BEFORE AND AFTER 1800

During the 18th century, goods were often manufactured in houses or small shops. With increased technology allowing for the use of machines, **factories** began to develop. In factories, a large volume of salable goods could be produced in a much shorter amount of time. Many Americans, including increasing numbers of **immigrants**, found jobs in these factories, which were in constant need of labor. Another major invention was the **cotton gin**, which significantly decreased the processing time of cotton and was a major factor in the rapid expansion of cotton production in the South.

DEVELOPMENT OF LABOR MOVEMENTS IN THE 1800S

In 1751, a group of bakers held a protest in which they stopped baking bread. This was technically the first American **labor strike**. In the 1830s and 1840s, labor movements began in earnest. Boston's masons, carpenters, and stoneworkers protested the length of the workday, fighting to reduce it to ten hours. In 1844, a group of women in the textile industry also fought to reduce their workday to ten hours, forming the **Lowell Female Labor Reform Association**. Many other protests occurred and organizations developed through this time period with the same goal in mind.

INDUSTRIALIZATION IN THE 19TH CENTURY

The Industrial Revolution in the United States lasted from 1820-1870. During that time, machines and factories took over the production of goods. These technologies allowed goods to be produced at a much faster rate so businesses could sell more products and make more money. Railroads lines were being expanded, so goods more easily could travel across the country to new markets. Industrialization changed life in the United States because the country shifted from an agricultural economy to an industrial economy. People moved to cities where the factories were and no longer worked on family farms. The Industrial Revolution turned the United States into a modern country.

Social Studies Skills

SOCIAL STUDIES SKILLS
COLLECTING INFORMATION AND ORGANIZING AND REPORTING RESULTS

The first step of compiling data for useful implementation requires narrowing down on a **topic**. The student should first read background information to identify areas that are interesting or need further study and that the student does not have a strong opinion about. The research question should be identified, and the student should refer to general sources that can point to more specific information. When he or she begins to take notes, his or her information must be **organized** with a clear system to identify the source. Any information from outside sources must be acknowledged with **footnotes** or a **bibliography**. To gain more specific information about his or her topic, the student can then research bibliographies from general sources to narrow down on information pertinent to the topic at hand. He or she should draft a thesis statement that summarizes the main point of the research. This should lead to a working **outline** that incorporates all the ideas needed to support the main point in a logical order. A rough draft should incorporate the results of the research in the outlined order, with all citations clearly inserted. The paper should then be edited for clarity, style, flow, and content.

FORMULATING RESEARCH QUESTIONS OR HYPOTHESES

Formulating research questions or hypotheses is the process of finding questions to answer that have not yet been asked. The first step in the process is reading **background information**. Knowing about a general topic and reading about how other people have addressed it helps identify areas that are well understood. Areas that are not as well understood may either be lightly addressed in the available literature or distinctly identified as a topic that is not well understood and deserves further study. Research questions or hypotheses may address such an unknown aspect, or they may focus on drawing parallels between similar, well-researched topics that have not been connected before. Students usually need practice in developing research questions that are of the appropriate scope so that they will find enough information to answer the question, yet not so much that they become overwhelmed. Hypotheses tend to be more specific than research questions.

IDENTIFYING MAIN IDEAS IN A DOCUMENT

Main ideas in a paragraph are often found in the **topic sentence**, which is usually the first or second sentence in the paragraph. Every following sentence in the paragraph should relate to that initial information. Sometimes, the first or second sentence doesn't obviously set up the main idea. When that happens, each sentence in the paragraph should be read carefully to find the **common theme** between them all. This common theme is the main idea of the paragraph. Main ideas in an entire document can be found by analyzing the structure of the document. Frequently, the document begins with an introductory paragraph or abstract that will summarize the main ideas. Each paragraph often discusses one of the main ideas and contributes to the overall goal of the document. Some documents are divided up into chapters or sections, each of which discusses a main idea. The way that main ideas are described in a document (either in sentences, paragraphs, or chapters) depends on the length of the document.

USING ELECTRONIC RESOURCES AND PERIODICALS FOR REFERENCE

Electronic resources are often the quickest, most convenient way to get background information on a topic. One of the particular strengths of **electronic resources** is that they can also provide primary-source multimedia video, audio, or other visual information on a topic that would not be accessible in print. Information available on the internet is not often carefully screened for accuracy or for bias, so choosing the **source** of electronic information is often very important. Electronic encyclopedias can provide excellent overview information, but publicly edited resources like Wikipedia are open to error, rapid change, incompleteness, or bias. Students should be made aware of the different types and reliabilities of electronic resources, and they should be taught how to distinguish between them. Electronic resources can often be too detailed and overwhelm students with irrelevant information. **Periodicals** provide current information on social science events, but they too must be screened for bias. Some amount of identifiable bias can actually be an important source of information, because it indicates prevailing culture and standards. Periodicals generally have tighter editorial standards than electronic resources, so completeness and overt errors are not usually as problematic. Periodicals can also provide primary-source information with interviews and photographs.

USING ENCYCLOPEDIAS, BIBLIOGRAPHIES, OR ALMANACS FOR SOCIAL SCIENCE RESEARCH

Encyclopedias are ideal for getting background information on a topic. They provide an overview of the topic and link it to other concepts that can provide additional keywords, information, or subjects. They can help students narrow their topic by showing the subtopics within the overall topic and by relating it to other topics. **Encyclopedias** may sometimes prove to be more useful than the internet because they provide a clearly organized, concise overview of material. **Bibliographies** are bound collections of references to periodicals and books, organized by topic. Students can begin researching more efficiently after they identify a topic, look it up in a bibliography, and look up the references listed there. This provides a branching network of information a student can follow. A pitfall of bibliographies is that when in textbooks or other journal articles, the references in them are chosen to support the author's point of view and so may be limited in scope. **Almanacs** are volumes of facts published annually. They provide numerical information on just about every topic, and are organized by subject or geographic region. They are often helpful for supporting arguments made using other resources and do not provide any interpretation of their own.

PRIMARY AND SECONDARY RESOURCES

Primary resources provide information about an event from the perspective of people who were present at the event. They might be letters, autobiographies, interviews, speeches, artworks, or anything created by people with first-hand experience. **Primary resources** are valuable because they provide not only facts about the event but also information about the surrounding circumstances; for example, a letter might provide commentary about how a political speech was received. The internet is a source of primary information, but care must be taken to evaluate the perspective of the website providing that information. Websites hosted by individuals or special-interest organizations are more likely to be biased than those hosted by public organizations, governments, educational institutions, or news associations. **Secondary resources** provide information about an event but were not written at the time the event occurred. They draw information from primary sources. Because secondary sources were written later, they have the added advantage of historical perspective, multiple points of view, or resultant outcomes. Newsmagazines that write about an event even a week after it occurred count as secondary sources. Secondary sources tend to analyze events more effectively or thoroughly than primary sources.

> **Review Video: What are Primary and Secondary Resources?**
> Visit mometrix.com/academy and enter code: 383328

ORGANIZING INFORMATION CHRONOLOGICALLY AND ANALYZING THE SEQUENCE OF EVENTS

To organize information chronologically, each piece of information must be associated with a time or a date. Events are ordered according to the time or date at which they happened. In social sciences, chronological organization is the most straightforward way to arrange information, because it relies on a uniform, fixed scale—the passage of time. Information can also be organized based on any of the "who, what, when, where, why?" principles.

Analyzing the sequence of chronological events involves not only examining the event itself but the preceding and following events. This can put the event in question into perspective, showing how a certain thing might have happened based on preceding history. One large disadvantage of chronological organization is that it may not highlight important events clearly relative to less important events. Determining the relative importance of events depends more strongly on interpreting their relationships to neighboring events.

RECOGNIZING CAUSE-AND-EFFECT RELATIONSHIPS AND COMPARING SIMILARITIES AND DIFFERENCES

Cause-and-effect relationships are simply linkages between an event that happened (the **effect**) because of some other event (the **cause**). Effects are always chronologically ordered after causes. Effects can be found by asking why something happened or looking for information following words like *so, consequently, since, because, therefore, this led to, as a result*, and *thus*. Causes can also be found by asking what happened. **Comparing similarities and differences** involves mentally setting two concepts next to each other and then listing the ways they are the same and the ways they are different. The level of comparison varies by student level; for example, younger students may compare the physical characteristics of two animals while older students compare the themes of a book. Similarity/difference comparisons can be made by listing written descriptions in a point-by-point approach, or they can be done in several graphic ways. Venn diagrams are commonly used to organize information, showing non-overlapping clouds filled with information about the different characteristics of A and B, and the overlapping area shows ways in which A and B are the same. Idea maps using arrows and bubbles can also be developed to show these differences.

DISTINGUISHING BETWEEN FACT AND OPINION

Students easily recognize that **facts** are true statements that everyone agrees on, such as an object's name or a statement about a historical event. Students also recognize that **opinions** vary about matters of taste, such as preferences in food or music, that rely on people's interpretation of facts. Simple examples are easy to spot. **Fact-based passages** include certainty-grounded words like *is, did*, or *saw*. On the other hand, **passages containing opinions** often include words that indicate possibility rather than certainty, such as *would, should*, or *believe*. First-person verbs also indicate opinions, showing that one person is talking about his or her experience. Less clear are examples found in higher-level texts. For example, primary-source accounts of a Civil War battle might include facts ("*x* battle was fought today") and also opinions ("Union soldiers are not as brave as Confederate soldiers") that are not clearly written as such ("I believe Union soldiers..."). At the same time that students learn to interpret sources critically (Was the battle account written by a Southerner?), they should practice sifting fact from these types of opinion. Other examples where fact and opinion blend together are self-authored internet websites.

> **Review Video: Fact or Opinion**
> Visit mometrix.com/academy and enter code: 870899

DETERMINING THE ADEQUACY, RELEVANCE, AND CONSISTENCY OF INFORMATION

Before information is sought, a list of **guiding questions** should be developed to help determine whether information found is adequate, relevant, and consistent. These questions should be based on the **research goals**, which should be laid out in an outline or concept map. For example, a student writing a report on Navajo social structure might begin with questions concerning the general lifestyle and location of Navajos and follow with questions about how Navajo society was organized. While researching his questions, he or she will come up with pieces of information. This information can be compared to his or her research questions to determine whether it is **relevant** to his or her report. Information from several sources should be compared to determine whether the information is **consistent**. Information that is **adequate** helps answer specific questions that are part of the research goals. Inadequate information for this particular student might be a statement such as "Navajos had a strong societal structure," because the student is probably seeking more specific information.

DRAWING CONCLUSIONS AND MAKING GENERALIZATIONS ABOUT A TOPIC

Students reading about a topic will encounter different facts and opinions that contribute to their overall impression of the material. The student can critically examine the material by thinking about what facts have been included, how they have been presented, what they show, what they relate to outside the written material, and what the author's conclusion is. Students may agree or disagree with the author's conclusion, based on the student's interpretation of the facts the author presented. When working on a research project, a student's research questions will help him or her gather details that will enable him or her to **draw a conclusion** about the research material.

Generalizations are blanket statements that apply to a wide number of examples. They are similar to conclusions but do not have to summarize the information as completely as conclusions. Generalizations in reading material may be flagged by words such as *all*, *most*, *none*, *many*, *several*, *sometimes*, *often*, *never*, *overall*, or *in general*. Generalizations are often followed by supporting information consisting of a list of facts. Generalizations can refer to facts or the author's opinions, and they provide a valuable summary of the text overall.

ABSOLUTE AND RELATIVE CHRONOLOGY

Chronology means arranging events in the order they occurred in time. A timeline is one common way of showing a chronology. Absolute chronology is based on a calendar. In an absolute chronology, events are located based on the day, month, or year they occurred and are organized from oldest to most recent. Relative chronology, on the other hand, is a chronology in which events are located relative to each other. The relationship of the events, rather than a calendar, is the organizational tool. A particular event is located based on when another event occurred. For example, event X occurred first, event Y occurred second, and event Z occurred third.

EVALUATING AND INTERPRETING MAPS

The **map legend** is an area that provides interpretation information such as the key, the scale, and how to interpret the map. The **key** is the area that defines symbols, abbreviations, and color schemes used on the map. Any feature identified on the map should be defined in the key. The **scale** is a feature of the map legend that tells how distance on the map relates to distance on the ground. It can either be presented mathematically in a ratio or visually with a line segment. For example, it could say that one inch on the map equals one foot on the ground, or it could show a line segment and tell how much distance on the map the line symbolizes. **Latitude** and **longitude** are often shown on maps to relate their area to the world. Latitude shows how far a location is north or south from Earth's equator, and longitude shows how far a location is east or west from Earth's prime meridian. Latitude runs from 90°N (North Pole) to 0° (equator) to 90°S (South Pole), and longitude runs 180°E (International Date Line) to 0° (prime meridian) to 180°W (International Date Line).

> **Review Video: 5 Elements of any Map**
> Visit mometrix.com/academy and enter code: 437727

POPULAR MAP PROJECTIONS

- **Globe**: Earth's features are shown on a sphere. No distortion of distances, directions, or areas occurs.
- **Mercator**: Earth's features are projected onto a cylinder wrapped around a globe. This generates a rectangular map that is not distorted at the equator but is greatly distorted near the poles. Lines of latitude and longitude form a square grid.
- **Robinson**: Earth's features are projected onto an oval-looking map. Areas near the poles are truer to size than in the Mercator. Some distortion affects every point.
- **Orthographic**: Earth's features are shown on a circle, which is tangent to the globe at any point chosen by the mapmaker. This generates a circular, 3D-appearing map similar to how Earth is seen from space.

- **Conic maps**: This family of maps is drawn by projecting the globe's features onto a cone set onto the globe. Some distortion affects most points.
- **Polar maps**: The land around the poles has been projected onto a circle. This provides much less distortion of Antarctica and the land around the North Pole than other map types.

CARTOGRAPHIC DISTORTION AND ITS INFLUENCE ON MAP PROJECTIONS

Cartographic distortion is the distortion caused by projecting a three-dimensional structure, in this case, Earth's surface, onto the two-dimensional surface of a map. Numerous map projections have been developed to minimize distortion, but the only way to eliminate distortion completely is to render Earth in three dimensions. Most map projections have minimal distortion in some location, usually the center, and the distortion becomes greater close to the edges of the map. Some map projections try to compromise and distribute the distortion more evenly across the map. Different categories of maps preserve, or do not distort, different features. Maps that preserve directions accurately are **azimuthal**, and maps that preserve shapes properly are **conformal**. Area-preserving maps are called **equal-area maps**, and maps that preserve distance are called **distance-preserving**. Maps that preserve the shortest routes are **gnomonic projections**.

> **Review Video: Map Projections**
> Visit mometrix.com/academy and enter code: 327303

COMPARING MAPS OF THE SAME PLACE FROM DIFFERENT TIME PERIODS

Maps of the same place from different time periods can often be initially aligned by **geographic features**. Political and land-use boundaries are most likely to change between time periods, whereas locations of waterways and geologic features such as mountains are relatively constant. Once geographic features have been used to align maps, they can be compared side-by-side to examine the changing locations of human settlement, smaller waterways, etc. This kind of map interpretation, at the smallest scale, provides information about how small groups of humans **interact with their environment**. For example, such analysis might show that major cities began around ports and then moved inland as modes of transportation, like railroads and cars, became more common. Lands that were initially used for agriculture might become incorporated into a nearby city as the population grows. This kind of map analysis can also show the evolution of the **socio-economics** of an area, providing information about the relative importance of economic activities (manufacturing, agriculture, or trade) and even the commuting behavior of workers.

NATURAL, POLITICAL, AND CULTURAL FEATURES ON MAPS

Map legends will provide information about the types of natural, political, or cultural features on a map. Some maps show only one of these three features. **Natural features** such as waterways, wetlands, beaches, deserts, mountains, highlands, and plains can be compared between regions by type, number, distribution, or any other physical characteristic. **Political features** such as state and county divisions or roads and railroads can be compared numerically, but examining their geographic distribution may be more informative. This provides information on settlement density and population. In addition, road and railroad density may show regions of intense urbanization, agricultural regions, or industrial centers. **Cultural features** may include roads and railroads, but might also include historic areas, museums, archaeological digs, early settlements, and even campgrounds. Comparing and contrasting the number, distribution, and types of these features may provide information on the history of an area, the duration of settlement of an area, or the current use of the area (for example, many museums are found in current-day cultural centers).

COMPARING MAPS WITH DATASETS OR TEXTS

Maps can provide a great deal of information about an area by showing specific locations where certain types of settlement, land use, or population growth occurred. **Datasets** and **texts** can provide more specific information about events that might only otherwise be hypothesized from maps. This specific information may provide dates of significant events (for example, the date of a fire that gutted a downtown region, forcing suburban development) or important numerical data (e.g., population growth by year). Written datasets and texts enable map interpretation to become concrete and allow observed trends to be linked with specific causes ("Real estate prices rose in 2004, causing middle-class citizens to move northwest of the city"). Without specific information from additional sources, inferences drawn from maps cannot be put in **context** and interpreted in more than a vague way.

EVALUATING AND INTERPRETING OTHER GRAPHIC FORMATS

The type of information being conveyed guides the choice of **format**. Textual information and numeric information must be displayed with different techniques. Text-only information may be most easily summarized in a diagram or a timeline. If the text includes numeric information, it may be converted into a chart that shows the size of groups, connects ideas in a table or graphic, or shows information in a hybridized format. Numeric information is often most helpfully presented in tables or graphs. When information will be referred to and looked up again and again, tables are often most helpful for the reader. When the trends in the numeric information are more important than the numbers themselves, graphs are often the best choice. Information that is linked to the land and has a spatial component is best conveyed using maps.

INTERPRETING CHARTS AND TABLES

Charts used in social science are a visual representation of data. They combine graphic and textual elements to convey information in a concise format. Often, **charts** divide the space up in blocks, which are filled with text and/or pictures to convey a point. Charts are often organized in tabular form, where blocks below a heading all have information in common. Charts also divide information into conceptual, non-numeric groups (for example, "favorite color"), which are then plotted against a numerical axis (e.g., "number of students"). Charts should be labeled in such a way that a reader can locate a point on the chart and then consult the surrounding axes or table headings to understand how it compares to other points. **Tables** are a type of chart that divides textual information into rows and columns. Each row and column represent a characteristic of the information. For example, a table might be used to convey demographic information. The first column would provide "year," and the second would provide "population." Reading across the rows, one could see that in the year 1966, the population of Middletown was 53,847. Tracking the columns would show how frequently the population was counted.

INTERPRET GRAPHS AND DIAGRAMS

Graphs are similar to charts, except that they graphically show numeric information on both axes. For example, a **graph** might show population through the years, with years on the x axis and population on the y axis. One advantage of graphs is that the population during the time in between censuses can be estimated by locating that point on the graph. Each axis should be labeled to allow the information to be interpreted correctly, and the graph should have an informative title.

Diagrams are usually drawings that show the progression of events. The drawings can be fairly schematic, as in a flow chart, or they can be quite detailed, as in a depiction of scenes from a battle. Diagrams usually have arrows connecting the events or boxes shown. Each event or box should be

labeled to show what it represents. Diagrams are interpreted by following the progression along the arrows through all events.

Review Video: Understanding Charts and Tables
Visit mometrix.com/academy and enter code: 882112

USING TIMELINES IN SOCIAL SCIENCE

Timelines are used to show the relationships between people, places, and events. They are ordered chronologically and usually are shown left-to-right or top-to-bottom. Each event on the **timeline** is associated with a date, which determines its location on the timeline. On electronic resources, timelines often contain hyperlinks associated with each event. Clicking on the event's hyperlink will open a page with more information about the event. **Cause-and-effect relationships** can be observed on timelines, which often show a key event and then resulting events following in close succession. These can be helpful for showing the order of events in time or the relationships between similar events. They help make the passage of time a concrete concept and show that large periods pass between some events, while other events cluster very closely.

USING POLITICAL CARTOONS IN SOCIAL SCIENCE STUDIES

Political cartoons are drawings that memorably convey an opinion. These opinions may be supportive or critical and may summarize a series of events or pose a fictional situation that summarizes an attitude. **Political cartoons** are, therefore, secondary sources of information that provide social and cultural context about events. Political cartoons may have captions that help describe the action or put it in context. They may also have dialogue, labels, or other recognizable cultural symbols. For example, Uncle Sam frequently appears in political cartoons to represent the United States government. Political cartoons frequently employ caricatures to call attention to a situation or a person. The nature of the caricature helps show the cartoonist's attitude toward the issue being portrayed. Every element of the cartoon is included to support the artist's point and should be considered in the cartoon's interpretation. When interpreting political cartoons, students should examine what issue is being discussed, what elements the artist chose to support his or her point, and what the message is. Considering who might agree or disagree with the cartoon is also helpful in determining the message of the cartoon.

Social Studies Practice Test #1

1. The three branches of government established by the US Constitution are divisions of the:
- a. Federal government
- b. Municipal government
- c. Regional government
- d. State government

2. The legislative branch of government is comprised of:
- a. Congress
- b. The House of Representatives
- c. State legislatures
- d. Senators

3. Broad Constructionists interpret the Constitution:
- a. Based on the Chief Justice's legal training
- b. In a manner that reflects the values of the justices
- c. Regarding the amendments as more important
- d. Valuing the states over the federal government

4. The first amendment guarantees all below except:
- a. Freedom of assembly
- b. The right to bear arms
- c. Freedom of the press
- d. The right to speak freely

5. Filibuster is a legislative procedure:
- a. Used to enact legislation quickly
- b. Used in the Supreme Court
- c. Used in the Senate
- d. Used by the President

6. Isolationism is a doctrine that says the US is best served staying out of foreign affairs and disputes. After the Revolutionary War, the US tried to maintain its isolationist strategy until:
- a. The Civil War
- b. The French and Indian War
- c. The Vietnam War
- d. World War I

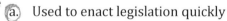

60

7. Which list of events is in the correct chronological order?

a.
• French and Indian War • American Revolution • French Revolution • War of 1812

c.
French and Indian War • French Revolution • War of 1812 • American Revolution

b.
• American Revolution • French Revolution • War of 1812 • French and Indian War

d.
French and Indian War • French Revolution • War of 1812 • American Revolution

8. The temperance movement in the US was related to:

   a. Abolition
   b. Civil disobedience
   c. Pacifism
   d. Revolution

9. Which of the following Supreme Court cases maintained the "separate but equal" practice of treatment toward racial minorities?

   a. Brown vs. Board of Education
   b. Marbury vs. Madison
   c. Plessy vs. Fergusson
   d. Roe vs. Wade

10. Westward migration during the 1800's in the US was catalyzed by:

   a. Overpopulation in the Northeastern US
   b. Precursors to interstate highways
   c. Potential economic opportunity
   d. Vigilantism by native peoples

11. Which of the following influenced the US Bill of Rights?

   a. The Magna Carta
   b. Martin Luther's 95 Theses
   c. Plato's Republic
   d. King James Bible

12. The US is a republic This means:

   a. Citizens vote directly on legislation
   b. Citizens elect representatives to voice their opinions
   c. Citizens elect a single leader to make decisions for the country
   d. Republicans run Congress

13. The Trail of Tears was:

   a. The forced removal of British soldiers after the American Revolution
   b. The forced evacuation of Cherokee peoples into Oklahoma
   c. The forced evacuation of freed slaves from the South after the Civil War
   d. The tears of Betsy Ross while she sewed the first American flag

14. Which of the following divided the North and South before the Civil War?

a. The Louisiana Purchase
b. The Mason-Dixon Line
c. The Mississippi River
d. The Continental Divide

15. The colony originally called New Amsterdam is now known as the state of:

a. Delaware
b. New York
c. North Carolina
d. Virginia

16. The Roanoke Colony:

a. Provided much evidence regarding colonial culture
b. Is also known as "the Lost Colony"
c. Befriended many native peoples
d. Established corn and wheat cultivation in the Americas

17. Lewis and Clark are known for exploring which region?

a. Appalachia
b. The Florida Keys
c. The Pacific Northwest
d. The Baja Peninsula of California

18. North American colonists grew cash crops, such as tobacco and cotton, primarily in what region?

a. The New England Colonies
b. The Central Plains
c. The Southern Colonies
d. The Wild West

19. Trade of rum, molasses, and slaves was among which three locales?

a. Africa, Canada, England
b. Africa, New England, West Indies
c. Africa, Canada, India
d. Amsterdam, Jamaica, South Africa

20. Modern, Federal Income Tax is an example of:

a. Congressional taxation
b. Presidential taxation
c. Progressive taxation
d. Represented taxation

62

21. A Writ of Habeas Corpus is a Latin phrase that translates literally to, "[We command] that you have the body." Prior to the American Revolution, English Parliament implemented this legal practice for trials in courts of law. The Habeas Corpus requirement is one right guaranteed to a defendant accused of committing a crime. Based on what you know about American civil liberties, as enumerated in the Bills of Rights, what does a Writ of Habeas Corpus ensure during a trial in a court of law in the US?

 a. That in a murder trial, the victim's body must be completely intact
 b. That a trial may not be held unless the accused is present
 c. That the accuser must be present to sentence the defendant
 d. That the judge must see the defendant before the trial begins

22. The Emancipation Proclamation resulted in:

 a. Slaves in Southern states immediately being freed
 b. Slaves in Union-controlled states being freed
 c. No new slaves being traded or purchased in the US
 d. Blacks given rights equal to whites

23. The industrial revolution was influenced by which of the following?

 a. Decrease in immigration
 b. Technological innovations
 c. Child labor restrictions
 d. Native American reconciliation

24. The House of Commons in English Parliament is similar to what entity in American Government?

 a. The House of Lords
 b. The House of Representatives
 c. The Presidential Cabinet
 d. The Supreme Court

25. Which box contains all the features of the rebel states during the Civil War?

a.
| Abolition |
| Blue Uniforms |
| Federal Governance |
| Northern States |

c.
| Abolition |
| Blue Uniforms |
| Federal Governance |
| Northern States |

b.
| Favored Slavery |
| Grey Uniforms |
| States Rights |
| Southern States |

d.
| No Stance on Slavery |
| Grey Uniforms |
| States Rights |
| Southern States |

26. Which of the following is true about the Gettysburg Address?

 a. Lincoln delivered the address at the onset of the Civil War.
 b. Emphasizes liberty as a founding principle of the US
 c. Was delivered at the Union's capital
 d. Gives the Rebels permission to leave the Union

27. Congressional districts are based on:

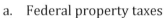

a. Percentage of free men in a state
(b.) Population density
c. Presidential appointment
(d.) Two representatives per state

28. Which of the founding fathers largely influenced the strength of the Federal Government?

a. Aaron Burr
(b.) Alexander Hamilton
c. Thomas Jefferson
d. John Hancock

29. McCullough vs. Maryland was a landmark Supreme Court case in which the state of Maryland was prohibited from imposing a tax on currency not issued by the state of Maryland: The decision sets a precedent for what principle?

a. Federal property taxes
b. Federally regulated currency
(c.) States rights
d. Printing currency on special paper

30. The French Revolution differs from the American Revolution by which of the following aspects?

a. Peaceful demonstration
b. Popular vote
(c.) Violent deposition of the monarchy
d. Philosophical ideology

31. Uncle Tom's Cabin by Harriet Beecher Stowe depicted the harsh life of slaves before the Civil War. Of the following novel titles, which likely contained a pro-slavery stance?

a. The African-American Experience
b. Huckleberry Finn
c. Narrative Life of Frederick Douglas
(d.) The Planter's Northern Bride

32. The "Underground Railroad" was primarily:

a. A route for abolitionists to smuggle weapons
b. A route for slave owners to traffic slaves
(c.) A means for slaves to travel to free states
d. A strategy for state control of railway construction

33. Which of the following differences between North and South during the Civil War was prominent in Lincoln's Gettysburg Address?

a. State vs. federal dominance
(b.) Slavery vs. abolition
c. Agrarian vs. industrial dependence
d. Urban vs. rural development

34. Which of the following contains congruous principals in the US between 1850 and1920?

a.	Slavery Prohibition Suffrage	c.	Abolition Prohibition States Rights
b.	Abolition Prohibition Suffrage	d.	Slavery Prohibition Municipal Rights

35. John Locke was a philosopher who influenced the founding fathers of the US. His essays, "A Letter Concerning Toleration" (1689) and "The Second Treatise On Civil Government" (1690), promoted separation of church and state and the rights of the individual. These principals are reflected in which of the following in the US?
 a. The Bill of Rights
 b. Checks and Balances
 c. The US Senate
 d. The Oath of Presidential Office

36. The religious philosophy Thomas Jefferson embraced was called:
 a. Atheism
 b. Authoritarianism
 c. Deism
 d. Polytheism

37. Which of the following is protected based on the principal of freedom of speech?
 a. City council decisions
 b. A pamphlet distributed by the Ku Klux Klan
 c. Martial law during a disaster
 d. State income tax

38. Colonial Puritans valued hard work and individual responsibility. These characteristics are evident in what aspect of the US economy?
 a. Free-market capitalism
 b. Income taxes
 c. Labor unions
 d. Welfare benefits

39. The concept of checks and balances is evident in which of the following?
 a. Federal judiciary appeals
 b. Presidential veto
 c. States rights
 d. The House and the Senate

40. The precedent for the two-term limit for the US Presidency was established by:

a. Abraham Lincoln
b. Alexander Hamilton
c. George Washington
d. Thomas Jefferson

41. George Washington's farewell address urged future Americans to:

a. Abolish slavery
b. Avoid foreign alliances
c. Encourage political party formation
d. Promote states rights

Questions 42 & 43 pertain to the following graph:

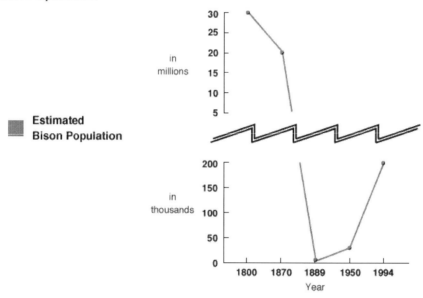

Bison Population

42. From 1800 to 1994, the Bison population in the US has:

a. Decreased from 30 million to 200
b. Stayed roughly the same
c. Decreased from 30 million to 200,000
d. Increased steadily

43. With what trend in American history did the bison population decreased to almost zero?

a. Construction of railroads in the southeastern US
b. The Civil War
c. The French and Indian War
d. Westward colonization

Question 44 pertains to the following map:

Largest Cities, 1900

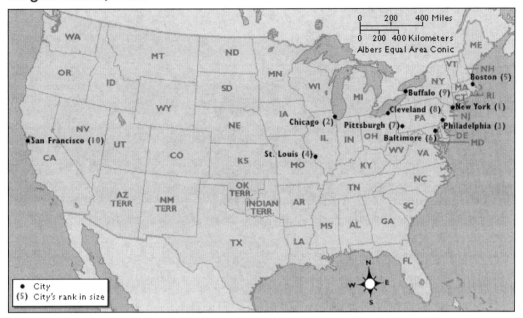

44. Which city is ranked 6th most populated?

a. Baltimore
b. Boston
c. Buffalo
d. Philadelphia

Questions 45-48 pertain to the following map:

Early European Settlements

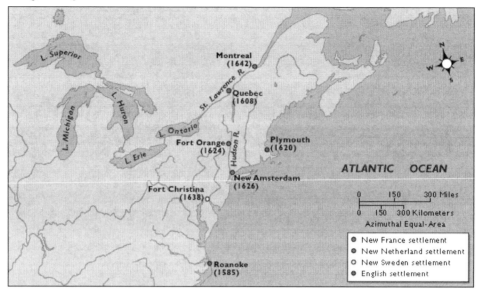

45. Which of the following is true about European colonization of the Americas?

 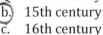

    a. France dominated early colonization
    b. England dominated early colonization
    c. Scandinavians did not colonize to the Americas
    d. Western European countries were equally represented in the Colonies

46. What geographic feature is shared by most of the colonies?

    a. Colonies were settled based on oceanic currents
    b. Colonies were settled in comfortable climates
    c. Colonies were settled on rocky areas
    d. Colonies were settled in ports

47. Which country had the first settlement in North America?

    a. Amsterdam
    b. The Netherlands
    c. France
    d. England

48. During which century did Colonists establish the first permanent settlement in North America?

    a. 14th century
    b. 15th century
    c. 16th century
    d. 17th century

Answer Key and Explanations for Social Studies Test #1

TEKS Standard §113.20(b)(3) and (15)(D)

1. A: The US Constitution specifies three branches of federal government. The legislative branch is comprised of Congress, and Congress is comprised of the House of Representatives and the Senate.

TEKS Standard §113.20(b)(15)(D)

2. A: The US Constitution specifies three branches of federal government. The legislative branch is comprised of Congress, and Congress is comprised of the House of Representatives and the Senate.

TEKS Standard §113.20(b)(18)(A)

3. B: Loose/Broad constructionist Supreme Court Justices interprets the Constitution as a malleable document and subject to interpretation relevant to the Justices' experience and legal precedent. Decisions made by broad constructionist Justices are sometimes accused of "legislation from the bench," meaning Justices may change laws, a job supposedly given only to Congress. Broad constructionists view themselves as watchdogs for ensuring the Constitutionality of laws passed by Congress.

TEKS Standard §113.20(b)(16)

4. B: The first amendment to the Constitution states, "Congress shall make no law respecting an establishment of religion, or prohibiting the free exercise thereof; or abridging the freedom of speech or of the press; or the right of the people peaceably to assemble, and to petition the Government for a redress of grievances." The right to bear arms is guaranteed by the second amendment: "A well regulated Militia, being necessary to the security of a free State, the right of the people to keep and bear Arms, shall not be infringed."

TEKS Standard §113.20(b)(15)(D)

5. C: A filibuster is a legislative practice outlined in the Constitution that may be used by a Senator to "wear out" his opponents, so to speak. Filibuster is threatened, but rarely used. Filibuster may be stopped by a three-fifths majority of Senators.

TEKS Standard §113.20(b)(5)(E)

6. D: George Washington warned against potential pit-falls he foresaw in the future of the US: political factions, foreign allegiances that might compromise the sovereignty of the US, and too much state control, among others. The avoidance of foreign allegiances resulted in isolationism being adopted as a practice until World War I. The US, in large part, stayed out of international conflict until World War I.

TEKS Standard §113.20(b)(1)(B)

7. A: The French and Indian War (Seven Years War) 1754-1763

American Revolution 1775–1783

French Revolution 1789–1799
The War of 1812 -1815

TEKS Standard §113.20(b)(24)(B)

8. A: The movement for abolition was linked with the movement for temperance due to the triangle slave trade of sugar & molasses, rum, and slaves. The temperance movement began with the aim to eliminate hard liquor, not wine and beer.

TEKS Standard §113.20(b)(18)

9. C: Plessy vs. Fergusson (1896) was a landmark Supreme Court case that prolonged civil rights discrimination against racial minorities. Homer Plessy challenged segregation on a railway car owned by John Howard Ferguson in Louisiana. The court ruled if facilities were equal for both races, segregation was legal.

TEKS Standard §113.20(b)(1)(A) and (6)

10. C: Because land was free or very inexpensive, and the Federal Government was giving monetary incentives to expand westward (The Homestead Act gave away over 800 million acres of land from 1862-1900 to anyone establishing a homestead at which to live for a minimum of 5 years), railroads and exploration were the driving forces.

TEKS Standard §113.20(b)(15)(A)

11. A: The Magna Carta (1215) is thought by historians to be the first recognition of individual rights, the major concept put forth in the Bill of Rights. Habeas Corpus and due legal process are manifestations of those individual rights identified in the Magna Carta that exist today in the Bill of Rights.

TEKS Standard §113.20(b)(15)

12. B: The US is a republic, meaning individuals directly elect representatives to voice their opinions in democratic processes and procedures. In a true democracy, individual citizens would debate and vote on legislation and policies.

TEKS Standard §113.20(b)(5)(G)

13. B: The Trail of Tears was the forcible removal of Native American tribes from their homes in the Southeastern US to Oklahoma. The name came due to the high number of Native Americans who died on the journey.

TEKS Standard §113.20(b)(7) and (8)

14. B: The Mason-Dixon Line, while established before the Civil War, was an effective line of demarcation between North and South during the Civil War. The line was originally a manifestation of a border dispute between Great Britain and the colonists.

TEKS Standard §113.20(b)(1) and (2)

15. B: New Amsterdam is now what we call New York City. It was called New Amsterdam by the majority Dutch settlers who initially colonized the area.

TEKS Standard §113.20(b)(1) and (2)

16. B: No evidence remains about the Roanoke Colony except that it did exist. Causes for its demise remain unknown.

TEKS Standard §113.20(b)(1)(A) and (6)

17. C: Meriwether Lewis and William Clark were the first to explore the Pacific Northwest region and Pacific coast beginning in 1806.

TEKS Standard §113.20(b)(7) and (11)(A) and (12)(A) and (12)(B)

18. C: Tobacco and cotton were the cash crops produced in the South. These were considered raw materials that could be shipped to the more industrial states to make finished products such as textiles and tobacco for smoking. The mild climate and moderate rainfall made this region ideal for growing these crops, in particular.

TEKS Standard §113.20(b)(12)(B)

19. C: The Triangle Slave Trade had the following stops: west coast of Africa for slaves, the West Indies for sugar or molasses and New England for manufacturing rum. These "commodities" were traded across nations and the triangle is a primary reason why prohibition and abolition were initially linked.

TEKS Standard §113.20(b)(15)

20. D: Americans pay federal income tax and elect officials to represent their interests in Congress and the Executive Branch of government. Taxes Americans pay is in proportion to their income and utilized to promote the interests of both majority and minority opinions.

TEKS Standard §113.20(b)(19)

21. B: A Writ of Habeas Corpus manifests in the accused person on trial in a court of law has the right to, and must be present to, defend himself for the trial to be held. The ideological roots of Habeas Corpus are in the Magna Carta.

TEKS Standard §113.20(b)(8)(b)

22. B: The Emancipation Proclamation (1863) effectively outlawed slavery in Northern States and made slavery illegal in states which were part of the Union. Southern states used this as fuel in their secession, in that they could not be in the Union and maintain slavery. The Union used the rebels' defiance to push southward in the battle theater during the Civil War.

TEKS Standard §113.20(b)(13)

23. B: Technological innovations such as interchangeable parts and the invention of the cotton gin catalyzed the industrial revolution in the second half of the 19th century. The pitfalls of child labor and unjust working conditions were part of the industrial revolution, but did not cause it. Immigration helped fuel the industrial revolution by providing a workforce.

TEKS Standard §113.20(b)(3)

24. B: The House of Commons is similar to the House of Representatives in that officials are elected by individuals to represent their interest in passing legislation.

TEKS Standard §113.20(b)(8)

25. B: Rebel states favored slavery, wore grey uniforms, favored states rights trumping federal law when the laws conflicted, and were the southern most states.

TEKS Standard §113.20(b)(8)(C)

26. B: Lincoln's Gettysburg Address (1863) inspired and reminded Union forces that the Union was founded on individual liberty, and the rebels were violating the most critical principle the Founding Fathers sought to protect.

TEKS Standard §113.20(b)(21)

27. B: Members of the House of Representatives from each state are proportionate in number to the state's population. Therefore, the House is the purest form of representative government in our federal system.

TEKS Standard §113.20(b)(15)(A) and (17)(A)

28. C: Alexander Hamilton authored the Federalist Papers, which favored federal supremacy over state laws and the importance of a strong federal branch of government leadership.

TEKS Standard §113.20(b)(18)(B)

29. B: In the case of McCullough vs. Maryland (1819) a majority ruled on the side of the federal government on the unconstitutionality of a state tax on non-state currency. This decision set the precedent for a centrally produced and regulated currency, which the US now has as the Federal Reserve.

TEKS Standard §113.20(b)(4)

30. C: French rebels executed the King and Queen of France. American rebels did stage a violent rebellion, but did not execute any of the British Monarchy or civilian Brits.

TEKS Standard §113.20(b)(26)

31. D: The Planter's Northern Bride was the most famous work of "Anti-Tom" literature following the publication of Uncle Tom's Cabin. The African-American Experience is a fictitious title, but suggests some objectivity or respect for black citizens of the US The Narrative Life of Frederick Douglas is the work of Douglas regarding the progress he led towards civil rights, beginning in 1845, before the Civil War.

TEKS Standard §113.20(b)(7)

32. C: The Underground Railroad was not necessary literally a railroad but a series of clandestine paths to move runaway and freed slaves out of Southern States prior to 1865.

TEKS Standard §113.20(b)(8)(C)

33. B: Lincoln stressed abolition as the focus in the Gettysburg Address.

TEKS Standard §113.20(b)(7) and (9)

34. B: Abolition, Prohibition, and Suffrage are linked via the Triangular Slave Trade and the reformation movements being led or supported by women.

TEKS Standard §113.20(b)(15)

35. A: The ideas and principals in John Locke's works from the late 17th century are reflected in the Bill of Rights: separation of church and state, free speech, and individual sovereignty.

TEKS Standard §113.20(b)(25)(A)

36. C: Deism posits that a Supernatural force created the world and universe, but that He did not intervene after creation. Jefferson wanted minimal central governing, as he viewed the Creator's relationship was with the universe.

TEKS Standard §113.20(b)(21)(B)

37. B: While abhorrent, a pamphlet written and distributed by a racist organization is permitted by the first amendment, the right to free speech.

TEKS Standard §113.20(b)(14)

38. A: Puritans valued self-sufficiency, hard work that would be rewarded by God in the after-life and on earth through success and in one's profession and family. Sins or laziness would be punished by lack of prosperity. The concept of survival of the fittest is congruent with capitalism: the best commodity will produce the most revenue, and inefficient production will cease. Free market capitalism, while secular, rewards performance.

TEKS Standard §113.20(b)(15)(D)

39. B: The President may veto legislation passed by Congress. The executive branch has this "check" on the legislative branch.

TEKS Standard §113.20(b)(3)

40. C: George Washington served 2 four-year terms as President. This interval of time was not specified in the Constitution, but future Presidents followed suit (until FDR).

TEKS Standard §113.20(b)(5)(E)

41. B: George Washington warned against potential pit-falls he foresaw in the future of the US: political factions, foreign allegiances that might compromise the sovereignty of the US, and too much state control, among others. Future presidents adopted his warning against foreign allegiances and kept the US largely out of international conflict until World War I.

TEKS Standard §113.20(b)(29)(C) and (29)(H)

42. C: The bison population was 30 million in 1800 and 200,000 in 1994.

TEKS Standard §113.20(b)(11)(B) and (29)(B)

43. D: Westward colonization via railroad lines facilitated bison hunting as a sport of frivolous loss. The bison population that existed before Americans moved westward was decimated, and has just in the past 20 years begun to replenish itself via conservation efforts by the Federal Government.

TEKS Standard §113.20(b)(29)(C) and (29)(H)

44. A: Baltimore is listed on the map as the 6th largest city.

TEKS Standard §113.20(b)(29)(C)

45. D: Western European countries were equally represented in the colonies, as is illustrated on the map.

TEKS Standard §113.20(b)(29)(C)

46. D: Colonies were settled in ports along the length of the eastern seaboard.

TEKS Standard §113.20(b)(29)(C)

47. D: England established Plymouth in 1620.

TEKS Standard §113.20(b)(29)(C)

48. D: Colonists established the first permanent settlement in North America during the 17th century.

Social Studies Practice Test #2

1. The three branches of government in the United States are called:

 a. Executive, legislative, and judicial
 b. Federal, state, and local
 c. National, constitutional, and representative
 d. Presidential, congressional, and legal

2. The three branches of federal government were enumerated in:

 a. The *Declaration of Independence*
 b. The first amendment
 c. The second amendment
 d. The *Constitution*

3. The first amendment is the first item in:

 a. The *Bill of Rights*
 b. The *Declaration of Independence*
 c. The *Emancipation Proclamation*
 d. The Writ *of Habeas Corpus*

4. The *Townshend Acts* of 1767 passed by British Parliament were:

 a. An attempt to provide representation of the colonies in Parliament
 b. An attempt to raise revenue following the Seven Years War
 c. An attempt to appease the demands of the Boston Tea Party
 d. An attempt to abide by the *Declaration of Independence*

5. The Seven Years War, called the French and Indian War by the Colonists:

 a. Was the precursor to the American Revolution
 b. Was a conflict related to European colonization
 c. Primarily took place in Canada
 d. Ended European conquests

6. Rum exported from _____ was made from sugar exported from the West Indies as a commodity in the West Indies slave triangle.

 a. Jamaica
 b. New England
 c. Southern France
 d. Western colonies

7. The *Magna Carta* influenced which of the following?

 a. Abolition
 b. The *Bill of Rights*
 c. Women's Suffrage
 d. The *Gettysburg Address*

75

8. Puritans fled Europe in order to:
    a. Become acquainted with potential native peoples
    b. Exercise freedom of the press
    c. Practice freedom of religion
    d. Reestablish the Holy Roman Empire

9. What type of leadership does the U.S. utilize?
    a. Monarchy
    b. Oligarchy
    c. Theocratic
    d. Republic

10. Cherokee people were forced out of the South during the mid-1800s. The forced evacuation is known as:
    a. The Appalachian Trail
    b. The Oregon Trail
    c. The Trail of Tears
    d. The Trail of No Return

11. What group of American colonists was led by William Penn, practiced pacifism, is also known as the Society of Friends, and believed in total equality among men?
    a. The Amish
    b. The Puritans
    c. The Quakers
    d. The Reformers

12. Guaranteed rights enumerated in the Declaration of Independence, possessed by all people, are referred to as:
    a. Universal rights
    b. Unalienable rights
    c. Voting rights
    d. Peoples' rights

13. Before the Civil War, to which of the following did Southern states object?
    a. An increase in Southern tobacco production
    b. An increase in tariffs on Northern manufactured goods
    c. An increase in western mining for gold
    d. An increase in the voting rights of slaves

14. The Mason-Dixon Line divided:
    a. The East from the West before the western states were incorporated
    b. The East from the West along the Mississippi River
    c. The North from the South before the Civil War
    d. The Senate from the House of Representatives

15. The 13 colonies did not include:

a. Delaware
b. Maine
c. South Carolina
d. Virginia

16. The American colony that left little evidence for historians was:

a. New Amsterdam
b. Norfolk
c. Roanoke
d. Williamsburg

17. The first successful English colony in the Americas was named for the English monarch who ruled during the early 1600s. A group of 104 English colonists settled in the Chesapeake Bay of modern-day Virginia, and initially befriended the Algonquin Indians. This colony was called:

a. New South Wales
b. New London
c. Jamestown
d. Georgeville

18. The Pacific Northwest was extensively explored by:

a. Mason and Dixon
b. Laurel and Hardy
c. Lewis and Clark
d. Washington and Jefferson

19. The mild climate and vast open spaces in the southern colonies were ideal for:

a. Large, industrial factories
b. Farming of a variety of cash crops
c. Growing flowers and making pottery
d. Railroad tracks and scenic tours

20. The Boston Tea Party was a protest against:

a. Being able to grow American tea
b. Being forced to drink tea in the Americas
c. Being taxed by England without being represented in Parliament
d. Being able to clean pollution out of Boston Harbor

21. The invention of interchangeable parts facilitated which of the following?

a. The American Revolution
b. The Feminist Revolution
c. The French Revolution
d. The Industrial Revolution

22. Southern plantation owners benefitted economically from which of the following?

    a. Freeing of slaves with the 13th amendment
    b. The invention of the cotton gin
    c. The American Revolution
    d. The invention of the automatic rifle

23. The Northern U.S. experienced economic growth during the 1800s largely as a result of:

    a. A new and continually growing railroad system
    b. The invention of the cotton gin
    c. Slavery
    d. Taxation

24. Freedom of speech is a right guaranteed by the *Constitution* in the *Bill of Rights*. What did early American colonists want to "speak freely" about, in particular?

    a. The King's Court
    b. The President
    c. Religious beliefs
    d. Slavery

25. Which entity in American government is the closest to direct democracy?

    a. The Electoral College
    b. The House of Representatives
    c. Committees within the Senate
    d. The Supreme Court

26. Which box contains all the features of the Union during the Civil War?

a.	Abolition Blue Uniforms Federal Governance Southern States	c.	Abolition Blue Uniforms Federal Governance Northern States
b.	No Stance on Slavery Grey Uniforms States Rights Northern States	d.	No Stance on Slavery Grey Uniforms States Rights Southern States

27. Alexander Hamilton's legacy is reflected in what quality of American government?

    a. Democracy
    b. Federalism
    c. Loose constructionism
    d. States rights

28. *Marbury vs. Madison* was a landmark Supreme Court decision that established the precedent of judicial review. Judicial review is congruous with which of the following aspects of U.S. government?

    a. Checks and balances
    b. Federalism
    c. Separation of church and state
    d. States rights

29. Thomas Paine was considered a propagandist prior to the American Revolution. Which of these is one of his famous works that influenced American political ideology?

    a. *Common Sense*
    b. The *Declaration of Independence*
    c. The Writ *of Habeas Corpus*
    d. The *US Constitution*

30. The illustration below is taken from a novel entitled *The Planter's Northern Bride*, a reactionary novel directed against Harriet Beecher Stowe's novel, *Uncle Tom's Cabin*. The *Planter's Northern Bride* is a novel categorized in the genre known as "Anti-Tom literature." The perspective of the novel is likely:

    a. Abolitionist
    b. Pro-slavery
    c. Romantic
    d. Baroque

31. After the Civil War, urban populations increased. This growth was likely due to:

    a. An increased reliance on agriculture
    b. The Industrial Revolution
    c. Prohibition
    d. Slavery persisting in some areas

32. The French Revolution took inspiration from the American Revolution. How do the revolutions differ?

   a. The central government established by the revolution
   b. The violent overthrow of a monarchy
   c. The style of battle
   d. The populist political ideals

33. John Locke was a philosopher who influenced whom?

   a. American businessmen during the industrial revolution
   b. The French Monarchy during the French Revolution
   c. The founding fathers of the U.S.
   d. Southern soldiers during the Civil War

34. Thomas Jefferson embraced a theological philosophy called deism, which promotes which of the following?

   a. Abolition
   b. Atheism
   c. Separation of church and state
   d. A theocratic central government

35. Which of the following is not protected under the principal of freedom of speech?

   a. Yelling "boo" during a Presidential address for laughs
   b. Yelling "fire" at a public gathering as a false alarm
   c. Yelling "vote for Lincoln" at a pro-slavery rally
   d. Not talking when taken into police custody

36. The economic structure of the U.S. is primarily a system of free market capitalism. From what group in American history is capitalism likely drawn?

   a. Colonial Puritans
   b. Native Americans
   c. States rights advocates
   d. Plantation owners

37. The presidential veto of legislation passed by Congress illustrates which principal in American government?

   a. Checks and balances
   b. Federal regulation
   c. Freedom of speech
   d. Separation of church and state

38. George Washington's farewell address and the *Monroe Doctrine* have which of the following in common

   a. Abolition
   b. Isolationism
   c. Presidential term limits
   d. Women's suffrage

39. The Articles of Confederation differ from the U.S. Constitution in what aspect?

a. Abolition of slavery
b. Federal deference to states rights
c. Judicial supremacy
d. Recognition of the British Throne

40. Representative democracy was likely motivated by:

a. An increase in population
b. Aristocracy
c. The Supreme Court
d. States passing laws that violated federal laws

Questions 41 – 44 pertain to the following map:

Agricultural Regions, 1900

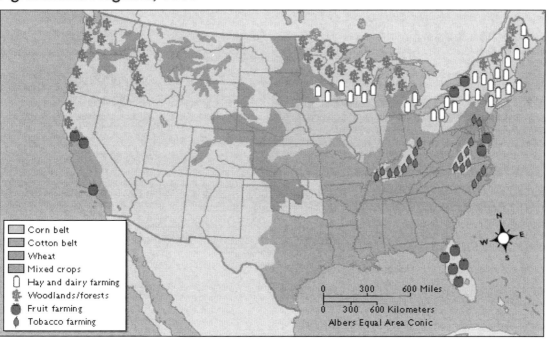

State	Inches of Rain per Year
California	17.28
Florida	49.91
New York	42.46

41. Which states were farming tobacco in 1900?

a. Florida, California, New York
b. Washington, Oregon, California
c. Kentucky, North Carolina, Virginia
d. Georgia, Alabama, Mississippi

42. Based on the map and the amount of rain per year, what can you extrapolate about fruit farming?

    a. Oranges are grown in California, Florida, and New York
    b. The amount of rain does not have an effect on fruit farming
    c. California, Florida, and New York each grow different fruits
    d. Nothing

43. What geographical feature related to average temperature do the woodland/forest areas share?

    a. Approximately the same latitude
    b. Approximately the same longitude
    c. Mostly Eastern states
    d. Mostly Western states

44. Approximately how wide, in miles, was the region of hay and dairy farming?

    a. 600 mi.
    b. 1,200 mi.
    c. 1,800 mi.
    d. 2,400 mi.

45. Passing of the *Homestead Act* resulting in the federal government giving out approximately 80 million acres of land from 1862 to 1900. What was the likely objective of the *Homestead Act*?

    a. To displace Native American peoples
    b. To encourage railroad construction
    c. To encourage western settlement and farming
    d. To create the Industrial Revolution

Questions 46 – 48 pertain to the following graph:

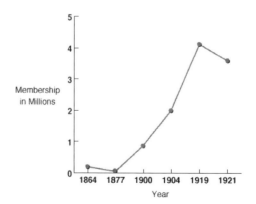

Union Membership, 1864–1921

46. Labor union membership increased in conjunction with what other development in American history?

    a. The Gold Rush
    b. The Civil War
    c. The Industrial Revolution
    d. A decline in manufacturing

47. Approximately how many people were members of labor unions in 1900?

    a. 1
    b. 1 million
    c. 10 million
    d. 100 million

48. What is a possible explanation for the sharp decrease in membership around 1919?

    a. Abolition
    b. More laborers were being treated fairly
    c. Fewer people trusted labor unions
    d. Prohibition

Answer Key and Explanations for Social Studies Test #2

TEKS Standard §113.20(b)(3) and (15)(D)

1. A: The *Constitution* lists three branches of federal government. They are the executive branch, the legislative branch, and the judicial branch.

TEKS Standard §113.20(b)(15)(D)

2. D: The *Constitution* lists the three branches of federal government.

TEKS Standard §113.20(b)(19)(B)

3. A: The first amendment is the first item in the *Bill of Rights*.

TEKS Standard §113.20(b)(4)(A)

4. B: The Seven Years War (called the French and Indian War by colonists) was very costly for the British government. In order to raise revenue, the British levied taxes on colonists. The colonists resisted, largely because they had no representation in British Parliament.

TEKS Standard §113.20(b)(1)(A)

5. B: The Seven Years War was a global military conflict. In the Americas, the conflict was largely between Western European countries, particularly Great Britain and France.

TEKS Standard §113.20(b)(12)(B)

6. B: The West Indies slave triangle's points are New England rum, West African slaves, and West Indies sugar or molasses.

TEKS Standard §113.20(b)(15)(A)

7. B: The *Magna Carta* is the first known mention of individual civil liberties as enumerated in the *Bill of Rights* of the *U.S. Constitution*.

TEKS Standard §113.20(b)(2)

8. C: Puritan colonists had been persecuted in Europe and sought religious freedom.

TEKS Standard §113.20(b)(3)

9. D: The U.S. is a republic: we elect representatives to vote on our behalf.

TEKS Standard §113.20(b)(5)(G)

10. C: The Trail of Tears was the forcible removal of Native American tribes from their homes in the Southeastern U.S. to Oklahoma. It was called such due to the high number of Native Americans who died on the journey.

TEKS Standard §113.20(b)(20)(A)

11. C: William Penn was a Quaker who settled what is now, Pennsylvania.

TEKS Standard §113.20(b)(19)(A)

12. B: "...endowed by their Creator with certain unalienable Rights," is excerpted from the Declaration of Independence. These rights are unable to be taken away from individuals, referring to the colonists' rights that Great Britain could not oppress.

TEKS Standard §113.20(b)(7)(A)

13. B: Southern states provided raw materials that were manufactured into commodities in Northern states. Southerners resented paying taxes to Northern states for these products (textiles, furniture, etc).

TEKS Standard §113.20(b)(7)

14. C: The Mason-Dixon Line was the manifestation of a border dispute between the British colonies of Pennsylvania, Maryland, and Delaware. It effectively separated, or illustrated a cultural divide between North and South before the Civil War.

TEKS Standard §113.20(b)(2) and (10)(A)

15. B: The 13 colonies were: Massachusetts, Rhode Island, Connecticut, New Hampshire, New York, Delaware, New Jersey, Pennsylvania, Virginia, Maryland, North Carolina, South Carolina and Georgia.

TEKS Standard §113.20(b)(10)(A)

16. C: There is no archeological or historical data of the Roanoke Colony, beyond that we know that there were colonists who settled there during the 17th century.

TEKS Standard §113.20(b)(1)(C) and (10)(A)

17. C: Jamestown was named for King James, and was the first colony of Great Britain to sustain itself.

TEKS Standard §113.20(b)(1)(A) and (6)

18. C: Meriwether Lewis and William Clark led the first expedition to the Pacific Northwest just after the turn of the 19th century.

TEKS Standard §113.20(b)(11)(A)

19. B: A temperate climate and moderate rainfall allowed for cotton and tobacco. Known as "cash crops," they were raw materials for manufactured goods such as textiles and tobacco smoking products, respectively.

TEKS Standard §113.20(b)(20)(C)

20. C: "Taxation without representation," is the infamous protest of colonists when they dumped tea into Boston Harbor. Great Britain levied many unjust taxes against the colonists, but the tax that "broke the camel's back," was the tax on black tea.

TEKS Standard §113.20(b)(27)(A)

21. D: The Industrial Revolution was catalyzed by assembly line production and interchangeable parts, e.g., those used to make the cotton gin and firearms invented by Eli Whitney. Manufacturing costs and time were drastically reduced with the advent of interchangeable parts.

TEKS Standard §113.20(b)(27)(A)

22. B: The cotton gin was particularly beneficial to Southern plantation owners because cotton was challenging to harvest and process manually. Cotton farmers could bring in a large crop to a local cotton gin to have it seeded and bailed.

TEKS Standard §113.20(b)(27)(D)

23. A: Railroads originating in the Northeast allowed manufactured goods to be exported to Southern states and Western territories.

TEKS Standard §113.20(b)(2)(B) and (3)(C) and (15)(D) and (25)

24. C: Religious persecution was an initial reason colonists fled to the Americas. By the time the *Bill of Rights* was written, the right to speak and write freely about government and religion were priority concerns.

TEKS Standard §113.20(b)(3)

25. B: Direct democracy is a system in which all members of a population vote directly on the issue at hand. A representative democracy refers to a system in which representatives vote on behalf of the population. The House of Representatives, the Senate, and the Electoral College are all representative democracies. The House of Representatives gives weight to population, whereas the Senate and the Electoral College do not. Members of the House of Representatives are elected in proportion to the population of each state. Representation by senators is not based on population and is therefore skewed in electoral weight. The Electoral College can and has contradicted the popular vote in the Presidential election.

TEKS Standard §113.20(b)(8)(B)

26. C: The Union was represented in blue military uniforms, was comprised of Northern states, generally supported abolition of slavery, and favored a central government that could trump laws passed by individual states.

TEKS Standard §113.20(b)(15)(A) and (17)(A)

27. B: Alexander Hamilton authored the *Federalist Papers* which later became the stance of the Union during the Civil War.

TEKS Standard §113.20(b)(18)(B)

28. A: The concept of checks and balances is manifested in the three branches of federal government and by the overlap of certain decisions by more than one branch. The President appoints the Supreme Court justices and reviews legislation passed by Congress. Judicial review is sometimes seen as the judiciary being activist or "legislating from the bench." However, the Supreme Court around the turn of the 19th century established the precedent that the Court could rule as unconstitutional, legislation it viewed was incongruous with the Constitution.

TEKS Standard §113.20(b)(4)(B)

29. A: Thomas Paine authored *Common Sense*, which argued for individual rights and against British oppression.

TEKS Standard §113.20(b)(26)

30. B: *Uncle Tom's Cabin* is the most famous abolitionist work of literature. There was some reactionary literature published after *UTC*, which presented arguments to preserve slavery, as it was not as horrific a picture as was painted by Northern intellectuals and non-slave owners. The illustration shows a white couple looking fondly at a kneeling black man, presumably slave. While the black man is in a subservient position, kneeling, he does not look like he has been mistreated.

TEKS Standard §113.20(b)(27)(B)

31. B: Growth of industry was concentrated in urban areas, which cyclically drew laborers into cities, growing the population of cities and increasing efficiency and quality in industry.

TEKS Standard §113.20(b)(4)

32. B: French rebels executed the King and Queen of France. American rebels did stage a violent rebellion, but did not execute any of the British monarchy or civilian Brits.

TEKS Standard §113.20(b)(20)(A)

33. C: John Locke was a 17th century philosopher who introduced many of the concepts embraced by the Enlightenment such as individual worth, knowledge gained by experience and empirical evidence. He also advocated for religious tolerance, separation of church and state, and the illegitimacy of monarchy.

TEKS Standard §113.20(b)(4)(B)

34. C: Thomas Jefferson embraced John Locke's concept of separation of church and state. Deism posits that a Supernatural force created the world and universe, but that He did not intervene after creation. Jefferson wanted minimal central governing, just as he viewed the Creator's relationship with the universe.

TEKS Standard §113.20(b)(19)

35. B: Freedom of speech, as mentioned in the *Bill of Rights,* does not include speech that is deceptive and causes others harm, e.g. yelling "fire!" when there is no fire in a crowded theatre.

TEKS Standard §113.20(b)(14)

36. A: Puritans valued self-sufficiency and hard work that would be rewarded by God in the after-life and on earth by success in one's profession and family. Sins or laziness would be punished by a lack of prosperity. The concept of survival of the fittest is congruent with capitalism: the best commodity will produce the most revenue, and inefficient production will be replaced.

TEKS Standard §113.20(b)(15)(D)

37. A: Presidents may veto legislation passed by both houses of Congress, and in turn Congress can override a presidential veto with a 2/3 majority. These governmental practices are a further

manifestation that each branch of government is watched by the other branches and, when necessary, can undo a decision it deems ill-advised or unconstitutional.

TEKS Standard §113.20(b)(5)(E)

38. B: George Washington warned against potential pit-falls he foresaw in the future of the U.S.: political factions, foreign allegiances that might compromise U.S. sovereignty of the, and too much state control, among others. Future Presidents adopted his warning against foreign allegiances which kept the U.S. largely out of international conflict until World War I.

TEKS Standard §113.20(b)(15)(B) and (15)(D)

39. B: The *Articles of Confederation* were the first attempt at a U.S. constitution. The *Articles* empowered the states much more than a central government. States rights would trump federal law under the *Articles*. This relationship was changed, of course, in the *Constitution*.

TEKS Standard §113.20(b)(3)

40. A: Representative government, by which citizens elect officials who share their views and who, in turn, present their views in a democratic system, is not a true democracy in which each individual votes on each issue. As the population of a democracy grows, the practicality of every individual voting on every issue becomes prohibitive to the process.

TEKS Standard §113.20(b)(29)(C) and (29)(J)

41. C: The map illustrates tobacco farming by the diamond-leaf shaped symbols in Kentucky, North Carolina, and Virginia.

TEKS Standard §113.20(b)(29)(C) and (29)(J)

42. C: Fruits are illustrated as being grown in California, New York, and Florida.

TEKS Standard §113.20(b)(29)(C) and (29)(J)

43. A: Woodlands and Forests are shown in the Pacific Northwest, North Central States, and Northeastern states. These states share the same range of latitudes as indicated on the map (as opposed to topography, rainfall, or some other influence on flora).

TEKS Standard §113.20(b)(29)(C) and (29)(H) and (29)(J)

44. C: Using the miles scale on the map, the hay and dairy region is approximately 1800 miles across.

TEKS Standard §113.20(b)(9)(D)

45. C: Passage of the *Homestead Act* encouraged people to move west by offering free or cheap land grants and/or money to begin a farm.

TEKS Standard §113.20(b)(29)(C) and (29)(D)

46. C: Labor unions began to form after the beginning of the Industrial Revolution as laborers began to suffer under the economic control of company owners. Laborers began to organize for individual rights in manufacturing settings such as safety, working hours, age of laborers, and

wages. Agricultural enterprises did not have the same density of workers or potential for dangerous work environments.

TEKS Standard §113.20(b)(29)(C) and (29)(H)

47. B: The y-axis of the graph shows approximately 1 million on the x-axis of 1900.

TEKS Standard §113.20(b)(29)(C) and (29)(D)

48. D: Prohibition during the 1920's coincided with the drop in labor union membership. Illegitimate manufacturing of alcohol and organized crime were counter to the formation of labor unions.

How to Overcome Test Anxiety

Just the thought of taking a test is enough to make most people a little nervous. A test is an important event that can have a long-term impact on your future, so it's important to take it seriously and it's natural to feel anxious about performing well. But just because anxiety is normal, that doesn't mean that it's helpful in test taking, or that you should simply accept it as part of your life. Anxiety can have a variety of effects. These effects can be mild, like making you feel slightly nervous, or severe, like blocking your ability to focus or remember even a simple detail.

If you experience test anxiety—whether severe or mild—it's important to know how to beat it. To discover this, first you need to understand what causes test anxiety.

Causes of Test Anxiety

While we often think of anxiety as an uncontrollable emotional state, it can actually be caused by simple, practical things. One of the most common causes of test anxiety is that a person does not feel adequately prepared for their test. This feeling can be the result of many different issues such as poor study habits or lack of organization, but the most common culprit is time management. Starting to study too late, failing to organize your study time to cover all of the material, or being distracted while you study will mean that you're not well prepared for the test. This may lead to cramming the night before, which will cause you to be physically and mentally exhausted for the test. Poor time management also contributes to feelings of stress, fear, and hopelessness as you realize you are not well prepared but don't know what to do about it.

Other times, test anxiety is not related to your preparation for the test but comes from unresolved fear. This may be a past failure on a test, or poor performance on tests in general. It may come from comparing yourself to others who seem to be performing better or from the stress of living up to expectations. Anxiety may be driven by fears of the future—how failure on this test would affect your educational and career goals. These fears are often completely irrational, but they can still negatively impact your test performance.

> **Review Video: 3 Reasons You Have Test Anxiety**
> Visit mometrix.com/academy and enter code: 428468

90

Elements of Test Anxiety

As mentioned earlier, test anxiety is considered to be an emotional state, but it has physical and mental components as well. Sometimes you may not even realize that you are suffering from test anxiety until you notice the physical symptoms. These can include trembling hands, rapid heartbeat, sweating, nausea, and tense muscles. Extreme anxiety may lead to fainting or vomiting. Obviously, any of these symptoms can have a negative impact on testing. It is important to recognize them as soon as they begin to occur so that you can address the problem before it damages your performance.

> **Review Video: 3 Ways to Tell You Have Test Anxiety**
> Visit mometrix.com/academy and enter code: 927847

The mental components of test anxiety include trouble focusing and inability to remember learned information. During a test, your mind is on high alert, which can help you recall information and stay focused for an extended period of time. However, anxiety interferes with your mind's natural processes, causing you to blank out, even on the questions you know well. The strain of testing during anxiety makes it difficult to stay focused, especially on a test that may take several hours. Extreme anxiety can take a huge mental toll, making it difficult not only to recall test information but even to understand the test questions or pull your thoughts together.

> **Review Video: How Test Anxiety Affects Memory**
> Visit mometrix.com/academy and enter code: 609003

Effects of Test Anxiety

Test anxiety is like a disease—if left untreated, it will get progressively worse. Anxiety leads to poor performance, and this reinforces the feelings of fear and failure, which in turn lead to poor performances on subsequent tests. It can grow from a mild nervousness to a crippling condition. If allowed to progress, test anxiety can have a big impact on your schooling, and consequently on your future.

Test anxiety can spread to other parts of your life. Anxiety on tests can become anxiety in any stressful situation, and blanking on a test can turn into panicking in a job situation. But fortunately, you don't have to let anxiety rule your testing and determine your grades. There are a number of relatively simple steps you can take to move past anxiety and function normally on a test and in the rest of life.

> **Review Video: How Test Anxiety Impacts Your Grades**
> Visit mometrix.com/academy and enter code: 939819

Physical Steps for Beating Test Anxiety

While test anxiety is a serious problem, the good news is that it can be overcome. It doesn't have to control your ability to think and remember information. While it may take time, you can begin taking steps today to beat anxiety.

Just as your first hint that you may be struggling with anxiety comes from the physical symptoms, the first step to treating it is also physical. Rest is crucial for having a clear, strong mind. If you are tired, it is much easier to give in to anxiety. But if you establish good sleep habits, your body and mind will be ready to perform optimally, without the strain of exhaustion. Additionally, sleeping well helps you to retain information better, so you're more likely to recall the answers when you see the test questions.

Getting good sleep means more than going to bed on time. It's important to allow your brain time to relax. Take study breaks from time to time so it doesn't get overworked, and don't study right before bed. Take time to rest your mind before trying to rest your body, or you may find it difficult to fall asleep.

> **Review Video: The Importance of Sleep for Your Brain**
> Visit mometrix.com/academy and enter code: 319338

Along with sleep, other aspects of physical health are important in preparing for a test. Good nutrition is vital for good brain function. Sugary foods and drinks may give a burst of energy but this burst is followed by a crash, both physically and emotionally. Instead, fuel your body with protein and vitamin-rich foods.

Also, drink plenty of water. Dehydration can lead to headaches and exhaustion, especially if your brain is already under stress from the rigors of the test. Particularly if your test is a long one, drink water during the breaks. And if possible, take an energy-boosting snack to eat between sections.

> **Review Video: How Diet Can Affect your Mood**
> Visit mometrix.com/academy and enter code: 624317

Along with sleep and diet, a third important part of physical health is exercise. Maintaining a steady workout schedule is helpful, but even taking 5-minute study breaks to walk can help get your blood pumping faster and clear your head. Exercise also releases endorphins, which contribute to a positive feeling and can help combat test anxiety.

When you nurture your physical health, you are also contributing to your mental health. If your body is healthy, your mind is much more likely to be healthy as well. So take time to rest, nourish your body with healthy food and water, and get moving as much as possible. Taking these physical steps will make you stronger and more able to take the mental steps necessary to overcome test anxiety.

Mental Steps for Beating Test Anxiety

Working on the mental side of test anxiety can be more challenging, but as with the physical side, there are clear steps you can take to overcome it. As mentioned earlier, test anxiety often stems from lack of preparation, so the obvious solution is to prepare for the test. Effective studying may be the most important weapon you have for beating test anxiety, but you can and should employ several other mental tools to combat fear.

First, boost your confidence by reminding yourself of past success—tests or projects that you aced. If you're putting as much effort into preparing for this test as you did for those, there's no reason you should expect to fail here. Work hard to prepare; then trust your preparation.

Second, surround yourself with encouraging people. It can be helpful to find a study group, but be sure that the people you're around will encourage a positive attitude. If you spend time with others who are anxious or cynical, this will only contribute to your own anxiety. Look for others who are motivated to study hard from a desire to succeed, not from a fear of failure.

Third, reward yourself. A test is physically and mentally tiring, even without anxiety, and it can be helpful to have something to look forward to. Plan an activity following the test, regardless of the outcome, such as going to a movie or getting ice cream.

When you are taking the test, if you find yourself beginning to feel anxious, remind yourself that you know the material. Visualize successfully completing the test. Then take a few deep, relaxing breaths and return to it. Work through the questions carefully but with confidence, knowing that you are capable of succeeding.

Developing a healthy mental approach to test taking will also aid in other areas of life. Test anxiety affects more than just the actual test—it can be damaging to your mental health and even contribute to depression. It's important to beat test anxiety before it becomes a problem for more than testing.

> **Review Video: Test Anxiety and Depression**
> Visit mometrix.com/academy and enter code: 904704

Study Strategy

Being prepared for the test is necessary to combat anxiety, but what does being prepared look like? You may study for hours on end and still not feel prepared. What you need is a strategy for test prep. The next few pages outline our recommended steps to help you plan out and conquer the challenge of preparation.

STEP 1: SCOPE OUT THE TEST

Learn everything you can about the format (multiple choice, essay, etc.) and what will be on the test. Gather any study materials, course outlines, or sample exams that may be available. Not only will this help you to prepare, but knowing what to expect can help to alleviate test anxiety.

STEP 2: MAP OUT THE MATERIAL

Look through the textbook or study guide and make note of how many chapters or sections it has. Then divide these over the time you have. For example, if a book has 15 chapters and you have five days to study, you need to cover three chapters each day. Even better, if you have the time, leave an extra day at the end for overall review after you have gone through the material in depth.

If time is limited, you may need to prioritize the material. Look through it and make note of which sections you think you already have a good grasp on, and which need review. While you are studying, skim quickly through the familiar sections and take more time on the challenging parts. Write out your plan so you don't get lost as you go. Having a written plan also helps you feel more in control of the study, so anxiety is less likely to arise from feeling overwhelmed at the amount to cover.

STEP 3: GATHER YOUR TOOLS

Decide what study method works best for you. Do you prefer to highlight in the book as you study and then go back over the highlighted portions? Or do you type out notes of the important information? Or is it helpful to make flashcards that you can carry with you? Assemble the pens, index cards, highlighters, post-it notes, and any other materials you may need so you won't be distracted by getting up to find things while you study.

If you're having a hard time retaining the information or organizing your notes, experiment with different methods. For example, try color-coding by subject with colored pens, highlighters, or post-it notes. If you learn better by hearing, try recording yourself reading your notes so you can listen while in the car, working out, or simply sitting at your desk. Ask a friend to quiz you from your flashcards, or try teaching someone the material to solidify it in your mind.

STEP 4: CREATE YOUR ENVIRONMENT

It's important to avoid distractions while you study. This includes both the obvious distractions like visitors and the subtle distractions like an uncomfortable chair (or a too-comfortable couch that makes you want to fall asleep). Set up the best study environment possible: good lighting and a comfortable work area. If background music helps you focus, you may want to turn it on, but otherwise keep the room quiet. If you are using a computer to take notes, be sure you don't have any other windows open, especially applications like social media, games, or anything else that could distract you. Silence your phone and turn off notifications. Be sure to keep water close by so you stay hydrated while you study (but avoid unhealthy drinks and snacks).

Also, take into account the best time of day to study. Are you freshest first thing in the morning? Try to set aside some time then to work through the material. Is your mind clearer in the afternoon or evening? Schedule your study session then. Another method is to study at the same time of day that you will take the test, so that your brain gets used to working on the material at that time and will be ready to focus at test time.

STEP 5: STUDY!

Once you have done all the study preparation, it's time to settle into the actual studying. Sit down, take a few moments to settle your mind so you can focus, and begin to follow your study plan. Don't give in to distractions or let yourself procrastinate. This is your time to prepare so you'll be ready to fearlessly approach the test. Make the most of the time and stay focused.

Of course, you don't want to burn out. If you study too long you may find that you're not retaining the information very well. Take regular study breaks. For example, taking five minutes out of every hour to walk briskly, breathing deeply and swinging your arms, can help your mind stay fresh.

As you get to the end of each chapter or section, it's a good idea to do a quick review. Remind yourself of what you learned and work on any difficult parts. When you feel that you've mastered the material, move on to the next part. At the end of your study session, briefly skim through your notes again.

But while review is helpful, cramming last minute is NOT. If at all possible, work ahead so that you won't need to fit all your study into the last day. Cramming overloads your brain with more information than it can process and retain, and your tired mind may struggle to recall even previously learned information when it is overwhelmed with last-minute study. Also, the urgent nature of cramming and the stress placed on your brain contribute to anxiety. You'll be more likely to go to the test feeling unprepared and having trouble thinking clearly.

So don't cram, and don't stay up late before the test, even just to review your notes at a leisurely pace. Your brain needs rest more than it needs to go over the information again. In fact, plan to finish your studies by noon or early afternoon the day before the test. Give your brain the rest of the day to relax or focus on other things, and get a good night's sleep. Then you will be fresh for the test and better able to recall what you've studied.

STEP 6: TAKE A PRACTICE TEST

Many courses offer sample tests, either online or in the study materials. This is an excellent resource to check whether you have mastered the material, as well as to prepare for the test format and environment.

Check the test format ahead of time: the number of questions, the type (multiple choice, free response, etc.), and the time limit. Then create a plan for working through them. For example, if you have 30 minutes to take a 60-question test, your limit is 30 seconds per question. Spend less time on the questions you know well so that you can take more time on the difficult ones.

If you have time to take several practice tests, take the first one open book, with no time limit. Work through the questions at your own pace and make sure you fully understand them. Gradually work up to taking a test under test conditions: sit at a desk with all study materials put away and set a timer. Pace yourself to make sure you finish the test with time to spare and go back to check your answers if you have time.

After each test, check your answers. On the questions you missed, be sure you understand why you missed them. Did you misread the question (tests can use tricky wording)? Did you forget the information? Or was it something you hadn't learned? Go back and study any shaky areas that the practice tests reveal.

Taking these tests not only helps with your grade, but also aids in combating test anxiety. If you're already used to the test conditions, you're less likely to worry about it, and working through tests until you're scoring well gives you a confidence boost. Go through the practice tests until you feel comfortable, and then you can go into the test knowing that you're ready for it.

Test Tips

On test day, you should be confident, knowing that you've prepared well and are ready to answer the questions. But aside from preparation, there are several test day strategies you can employ to maximize your performance.

First, as stated before, get a good night's sleep the night before the test (and for several nights before that, if possible). Go into the test with a fresh, alert mind rather than staying up late to study.

Try not to change too much about your normal routine on the day of the test. It's important to eat a nutritious breakfast, but if you normally don't eat breakfast at all, consider eating just a protein bar. If you're a coffee drinker, go ahead and have your normal coffee. Just make sure you time it so that the caffeine doesn't wear off right in the middle of your test. Avoid sugary beverages, and drink enough water to stay hydrated but not so much that you need a restroom break 10 minutes into the test. If your test isn't first thing in the morning, consider going for a walk or doing a light workout before the test to get your blood flowing.

Allow yourself enough time to get ready, and leave for the test with plenty of time to spare so you won't have the anxiety of scrambling to arrive in time. Another reason to be early is to select a good seat. It's helpful to sit away from doors and windows, which can be distracting. Find a good seat, get out your supplies, and settle your mind before the test begins.

When the test begins, start by going over the instructions carefully, even if you already know what to expect. Make sure you avoid any careless mistakes by following the directions.

Then begin working through the questions, pacing yourself as you've practiced. If you're not sure on an answer, don't spend too much time on it, and don't let it shake your confidence. Either skip it and come back later, or eliminate as many wrong answers as possible and guess among the remaining ones. Don't dwell on these questions as you continue—put them out of your mind and focus on what lies ahead.

Be sure to read all of the answer choices, even if you're sure the first one is the right answer. Sometimes you'll find a better one if you keep reading. But don't second-guess yourself if you do immediately know the answer. Your gut instinct is usually right. Don't let test anxiety rob you of the information you know.

If you have time at the end of the test (and if the test format allows), go back and review your answers. Be cautious about changing any, since your first instinct tends to be correct, but make sure you didn't misread any of the questions or accidentally mark the wrong answer choice. Look over any you skipped and make an educated guess.

At the end, leave the test feeling confident. You've done your best, so don't waste time worrying about your performance or wishing you could change anything. Instead, celebrate the successful

completion of this test. And finally, use this test to learn how to deal with anxiety even better next time.

Important Qualification

Not all anxiety is created equal. If your test anxiety is causing major issues in your life beyond the classroom or testing center, or if you are experiencing troubling physical symptoms related to your anxiety, it may be a sign of a serious physiological or psychological condition. If this sounds like your situation, we strongly encourage you to seek professional help.

Thank You

We at Mometrix would like to extend our heartfelt thanks to you, our friend and patron, for allowing us to play a part in your journey. It is a privilege to serve people from all walks of life who are unified in their commitment to building the best future they can for themselves.

The preparation you devote to these important testing milestones may be the most valuable educational opportunity you have for making a real difference in your life. We encourage you to put your heart into it—that feeling of succeeding, overcoming, and yes, conquering will be well worth the hours you've invested.

We want to hear your story, your struggles and your successes, and if you see any opportunities for us to improve our materials so we can help others even more effectively in the future, please share that with us as well. **The team at Mometrix would be absolutely thrilled to hear from you!** So please, send us an email (support@mometrix.com) and let's stay in touch.

If you'd like some additional help, check out these other resources we offer for your exam:

http://MometrixFlashcards.com/STAAR

Additional Bonus Material

Due to our efforts to try to keep this book to a manageable length, we've created a link that will give you access to all of your additional bonus material:

mometrix.com/bonus948/staarg8socst